PRAIS

WE are
ADAM

"Ramona Siddoway has given us a beautiful glimpse inside the Garden of Eden! With dozens of insights into the original Hebrew origins and insightful connections to modern Latter-day teachings, this book brings the story of Adam and Eve to life in a new and important way. If you are ready to take the story of Adam and Eve to a deeper level and better understand the power of men and women in God's plan, this book is for you!"

—Heather Ferrell, author, *Women in the Scriptures* series

"Ramona Siddoway's book, *We Are Adam*, is a wonderful and wide-ranging introduction to how the restored gospel of Jesus Christ beckons us as men and women to live as equal partners in the home, community, and Church. As a student not only of ancient scripture but of the modern prophetic voice, Siddoway's exegesis is profoundly insightful, and I highly recommend it."

—Valerie M. Hudson, author; University Distinguished Professor, Professor and George H. W. Bush Chair; Director Program on Women, Peace, and Security; Department of International Affairs The Bush School of Government and Public Service

"We Are Adam, well-researched and engaging, is an excellent step in the essential journey toward seeing female and male as equal partners—in the Garden of Eden, in the relationship of our Father and Mother in Heaven, and hopefully in the interactions of us all, in our sense of self, our marriages, our church, and our society. May this book reach many good hands and enlighten many good minds."

—Carol Lynn Pearson, author of *Finding Mother God: Poems to Heal the World*, *My Turn on Earth*, and *Goodbye, I Love You*

"This book presents a doctrinally thorough and correct understanding of our first mother, Eve. On such an important subject, because we are all sons of Adam or daughters of Eve, it is crucial to learn about our first mother from someone who truly supports, sustains, and follows the living prophets, seers, and revelators as our connection with heaven. Ramona treats the subject of divine womanhood with the reverence it deserves and the scripturally correct explanation that so many lack. If you are looking to understand feminism as I believe heaven intended, we can't afford to look to society. We must look to the scriptures and the inspired words of our leaders. This book does exactly that."

—Mark A. Shields, author of *Your Endowment*, *Gospel Symbols*, and others; father of five daughters

"Ramona Siddoway brings new life to one of the most beloved stories of the Old Testament in Adam and Eve, providing valuable insights that will enrich the spiritual journeys of men and women in our modern day. Even the most ardent Biblical scholars will gather fresh perspectives, while those who desire a deeper understanding of the spiritual power of women will find unchartered paths to personal revelation. Truly a work worth reading, pondering, and acting upon."

—Eric Shuster, author of *Where Are the Christians?*

WE *are* ADAM

THE PARTNERSHIP OF ADAM AND EVE IN THE GARDEN OF EDEN AND WHAT IT MEANS FOR YOU

RAMONA SIDDOWAY

CFI
An imprint of Cedar Fort, Inc.
Springville, Utah

ISBN 13: 978-1-4621-3824-1

Published by CFI, an imprint of Cedar Fort, Inc.
2373 W. 700 S., Springville, UT, 84663
Distributed by Cedar Fort, Inc., www.cedarfort.com

Library of Congress Control Number: 2020942575

Cover design by Wes Wheeler
Cover design © 2020 Cedar Fort, Inc.

Printed in the United States of America

10 9 8 7 6 5 4 3 2 1

Printed on acid-free paper

For my children,
Rachel, Sara, Lis, and Joseph.
Each of you have had a profound impact on
the creation of this book.

And most important, for Bryant,
my biggest cheerleader,
my partner in this crazy life,
the one who makes our life Eden.

CONTENTS

A NOTE FROM
THE AUTHOR

It is no accident that the prophet in these latter days raised no less than nine daughters. If there ever was a man who has been prepared and understands the hearts of women, it is President Russell M. Nelson. Truly, we are in an exciting restorative time, especially as it concerns the women of The Church of Jesus Christ of Latter-day Saints.

Through researching scriptures, apostle and prophet commentaries, and various Latter-day Saint writers, I address misunderstandings about women, partnership template in the Garden of Eden, priesthood, and the patriarchal order.

To truly understand Mother Eve, women, and their role in the patriarchal order, we begin with the foundational promise of the gospel. What is our true purpose here, and do we have enough trust in Heavenly Father that He will assist us in realizing the potential He has in mind for our individual lives?

At the conclusion of this book, the reader will have a better understanding and greater peace about specific genders, roles, and priesthood identity.

This book does not constitute official Church doctrine, and all opinions are mine. This book is a venue to illuminate the beautiful partnership that can exist between men, women, and God. Many of the quotes in this book are openly published by The Church of Jesus Christ of Latter-day Saints and will be discussed generally.

Other quotes are from apocryphal sources. I ask the reader to take them with a grain of salt and enjoy their possibilities. It's wise to remember the revelation given to Joseph Smith when he questioned the Lord about the Apocrypha, recorded in Doctrine and Covenants 91:1, 5: "Verily, thus saith the Lord unto you concerning the Apocrypha—There are many things contained therein that are true, and it is mostly translated correctly; And whoso is *enlightened by the Spirit* shall obtain benefit therefrom."

Asking questions and getting answers through the Spirit, and going to the right sources, comprise the foundation of gaining a correct testimony. It is not just *what* questions we ask, but the *intent,* that matters. Being driven with unity and respect in mind and having a sincere desire to know truth will invite the Holy Ghost.

The touchstones I have used throughout this manuscript have been the canonical scriptures, the words of modern-day prophets and apostles, as well as petitioning the Spirit. Many hours have been spent in the temple, both as a worker and patron, with this manuscript at the forefront of my mind. My focus has always been to bring comfort, peace, and information to those who question. Because of this, my testimony about the priesthood and the role of women has increased exponentially.

Without a doubt, I have discovered that God is good. We humans are not an experiment gone wrong. We are gods in embryo who will most certainly succeed by following His plan and trusting in the process.

Chapter 1
IN THE BEGINNING

*You keep using that word. I don't
think it means what you
think it means.*

—Inigo Montoya, *The Princess Bride*

EVE'S BEGUILEMENT

At the heart of any Judeo-Christian religion is a very specific garden. Nearly every human knows the central characters in that garden, whether or not that person believes they existed. Any child in Sunday School can repeat what transpired, why, and by whom. This origin story is tightly woven into our culture, affecting every relationship between males and females, as well as the roles they inherit.

To explore a woman's role in any type of priesthood capacity, we must first unpack some very deeply embedded cultural and Judeo-Christian misconceptions that go back to, what many consider, the beginning.

Throughout history, and still prevalent in some cultures today, is the stilted view of Eve's part in the Fall and her subsequent place in humanity. People have taken certain scriptures from Paul (see 1 Timothy 2:12–14 and 1 Corinthians 14:34, 35) to condemn Eve,

1

building a false foundation for Eve and her daughters' supposed inferiority and subordination to man. Two such arguments made are that Eve is inferior because (1) the serpent beguiled her and (2) she was made after Adam.

Let's first discuss the correct meaning of the word *beguile*.

The 1828 edition of Webster's Dictionary defines *beguile* as "to delude, to deceive, or to impose on by artifice or craft."[1] Webster's even quotes Genesis 3:13 as an example of the word. Eve's perceived mistake was definitely baked into the culture of the day. Because of this tradition, many believe that *beguile* simply means to be tricked or deceived.

Culture often creates subtle overlays in a group's dynamics. The specific doctrine on a topic may be entirely different than what is actually played out within a group. Culture also comes into play with certain translations. The translators of the King James Version of the Bible were all steeped in a philosophy of "original sin" beliefs and practices.

But Dr. Nehama Aschkenasy, a Hebrew scholar, writes that when accounting for her actions, Eve chose an uncommon Hebrew verb. He writes that *beguiled* "has retained an extraordinary flavor in Hebrew and is only used on rare and unusual occasions. Translations that opt for 'deceive' or 'trick' (instead of 'beguiled') lose the wealth and innovation of the woman's lexicon."[2]

Dr. Aschkenasy goes on to explain that Eve's choice to eat of the fruit was after (and through) intense, puzzling contemplation that involved Eve questioning and pondering her role—not only in the garden but also for eternity. Eve was not tricked into eating the fruit in the sense that she did so blindly. Eve began questioning the possible purpose of the tree—a gateway to greater intellectual capacity and a possible future that was closer to what the Father is living. By using this verb, Eve described the internal, mental process that took place before she ate the fruit.

A truer translation of *beguile* is much more complex and rich than the merely base, damning, and culturally tainted one of *tricked*. The latter creates a mental image of a weaker, less intelligent Eve in the minds of the readers, where, if the Hebrew lexicon of her language is studied, we find quite the opposite.

Another translation of Genesis 3:13 reads, "And the woman replied, 'The serpent caused me to feel responsible/guilty and I ate.'"[3] What did she feel responsible for? Perhaps Eve felt responsible for the fact that they were childless, that she was barren, and Satan insinuated that it was her fault.[4] "Through her elegant wording," wrote Dr. Aschkenasy, "the woman has lifted her disobedience to the level of a momentous event of great mental and existential significance."[5]

MOTIVES

It's not just what Satan *did* say when he communicated with Eve, but what he *didn't* say that made his claims deceptive. He claimed she wouldn't die. But she certainly would, and she would suffer much on the way to death. He also failed to mention the part about the big chunk of work ahead of her, leaving out everything that came in between eating the fruit and becoming like God.

Isn't that how he tempts any of us? He never provides us with—and didn't with Eve—the full story. He uses what we desire most as bait, promises a shortcut, and then distracts us from the unpleasant consequences.[6]

This situation, and all others that involve Satan, can be more clearly put into context when we consider the source and examine his motives. As we try to comprehend Eve's character, we cannot ignore Satan's.

Satan's entire mission has been an attempt to dethrone Father in Heaven as our God. Satan wants to be worshiped.[7] He wants the glory, the kudos, the followers, the throne. He wants the power without the responsibility. Just as there have been other worlds,[8] other "Adams,"[9] other "Eves," there must have been a template plan that was devised for each. We do not know the history of other worlds; we only know the dealings of God with this world and our history.[10] But Satan knew enough to believe that he had to get to the first parents and disrupt something of the plan. What was his motive? To be worshiped as he witnessed our Father in Heaven was worshiped.

The being who wants to be the god of this world suggested to Adam and Eve to put on flimsy, degradable leaves; not for protection but rather to cover—and ironically—highlight their shame, whereas our true God provides durable, long lasting animal skins,[11] garments of honor[12] and glory, a symbol of the full and protective covering of Christ's Atonement.

CONTEXT IS KING

Let's look at another contextual example of *beguile* from the Book of Mormon. Ammon, after he rescued King Lamoni's sheep in a heroic show of bravery, now has the king's ear. Lamoni asks him a question, and Ammon responds: "Wilt thou hearken unto my words, if I tell thee by what power I do these things? And this is the thing that I desire of thee. And the king answered him, and said: Yea, I will believe all thy words. And thus he was *caught with guile.*"[13]

No one would suggest that Ammon tried to trick or deceive Lamoni. But this verse and the dialogue between these two figures serves as an example as to the proper *flavoring* of the word *beguile.*[14]

But let us be clear: Ammon was harmless, whereas Satan certainly was and is not. The word is the same; the motives are entirely different.

SIN VERSUS TRANSGRESSION AND THE REAL CHOICE IN THE GARDEN

The Genesis version of the Fall records that the commandment not to partake of the fruit of the tree of good and evil was given to Adam alone. Adam consequently took it upon himself to relay that commandment to Eve, although it is not certain that he was instructed by Elohim to do so. The Hebrew in the Genesis account has "the commandment [as] directed to a second-person male—'you, man.'"[15] Within this specific narrative, it appears not as a commandment directed at Eve, but only Adam. However, as Latter-day Saints, we do have other renderings[16] of this story, allegorical as well in nature. But as we read the additional personal accounts of Adam *and* Eve, we see that both of them recognize and admit that by partaking, they were *transgressing* a commandment.[17]

Explaining the distinction between a sin and a transgression, Elder Dallin H. Oaks wrote:

> This suggested contrast between a *sin* and a *transgression* reminds us of the careful wording in the second article of faith: "We believe that men will be punished for their own *sins,* and not for Adam's *transgression*" (emphasis added). It also echoes a familiar distinction in the law. Some acts, like murder, are crimes because they are inherently wrong. Other acts, like operating without a license, are crimes only because they are legally prohibited. Under these distinctions, the act that produced the Fall was not a sin—inherently wrong—but a transgression—wrong because it was formally prohibited. These words are not always used to denote something different, but this distinction seems meaningful in the circumstances of the Fall.[18]

We can tell that Eve, by her comments made later, knew of what she did. It is erroneous to think that a plan as grand as the Father's had to be inaugurated with and by craftiness and trickery. Both Adam and Eve knew of the two commandments: 1) to multiply and replenish the earth and 2) not to partake of the fruit.

God gave them a choice: remain forever as they were in the garden (do not eat the fruit), or replenish the earth with children (eat the fruit) and leave the garden. As the garden was in a state of timelessness, no children could be conceived or born, as both conception and birth are required to have a forward movement of time. As death was not possible, neither was a true meaning of life. And just as birth and death were not possible, any other opposites were equally impossible. By partaking of the fruit, Adam and Eve introduced opposites: birth and death, happiness and sorrow. In other words, life.

Both knew what they wanted and what needed to be done. Life in the garden for Eve was not bearable without children, and for Adam, the garden was not paradise without Eve.

ENDNOTES

1. Websters Dictionary 1828, webstersdictionary1828.com/Dictionary/Beguile, accessed October 8, 2019.

2. Aschkenasy Nehama, "Woman at the Window: Biblical Tales of Oppression and Escape." Essay. In *Woman at the Window: Biblical Tales of Oppression and Escape*, (S.l., MI: Wayne State University Press., 1998), 128.

3. Shira Halevi, "The Life Story of Adam and Havah: a New Targum of Genesis 1:26–5:5." In *The Life Story of Adam and Havah: a New Targum of Genesis 1:26–5:5* (Aronson, 1997), 202.

4. Isn't that the tactic he usually uses?

5. Aschkenasy, 128.

6. 1 Nephi 8:23–24

7. Moses 1:12–19

8. Moses 1:33, 7:30

9. Moses 1:34

10. Moses 1:35

11. Moses 4:27; Genesis 3:21. See also Halevi, 13–15.

12. Halevi, 15. What is also fascinating here is how words can be translated and defined in Hebrew. According to Halevi, some translators wrote that God clothed Adam and Eve in garments of light or glory; and that light is a metaphor for knowledge, revelation, or joy. These garments, whatever their material, were worn next to the skin.

13. Alma 18:22–23, emphasis added.

14. The word *guile* as used in this scripture is a noun suggesting cunning, artifice, craft, and is most often used in a negative connotation. *Beguile* as used by Eve is a transitive verb of "be" and "guile" meaning to delude, impose, or deceive *by* craft or artifice. See webstersdictionary1828.com/Dictionary/Guile and webstersdictionary1828.com/Dictionary/Beguile

15. Halevi, 174

16. Latter-day temples

17. 2 Nephi 2:22–25; Moses 5:10–11

18. Dallin H. Oaks, "The Great Plan of Happiness," *Ensign*, November 1993.

Chapter 2
CURSES, CONSEQUENCES, AND COMPASSION

Wherefore, he gave commandments unto men, they having first transgressed the first commandments as to things which were temporal, and becoming as gods, knowing good from evil, placing themselves in a state to act, or being placed in a state to act according to their wills and pleasures, whether to do evil or to do good.

—Alma 12:31

Another of the biggest cultural misunderstandings that permeates and saturates the mainstream Christian culture is the idea of Eve's curse. Somehow, stereotypes have been carefully handed down through the generations, idioms passed down from mother to daughter, like a judiciously wrapped family heirloom. However, a careful reading of Genesis reveals that there were *two* curses pronounced in the garden and that neither Adam *nor* Eve was the recipient.

The account in Genesis 3 reads as follows (emphasis added):

> And the Lord God said unto the serpent, Because thou hast done this, *thou art cursed* above all cattle, and above every beast

of the field; upon thy belly shalt thou go, and dust shalt thou eat all the days of thy life:

And I will put enmity between thee and the woman, and between thy seed and her seed; it shall bruise thy head, and thou shalt bruise his heel.

Unto the woman he said, I will greatly multiply thy sorrow and thy conception; in sorrow thou shalt bring forth children; and thy desire shall be to thy husband, and he shall rule over thee.

And unto Adam he said, Because thou hast hearkened unto the voice of thy wife, and hast eaten of the tree, of which I commanded thee, saying, Thou shalt not eat of it: *cursed is the ground* for thy sake; in sorrow shalt thou eat of it all the days of thy life;

Thorns also and thistles shall it bring forth to thee; and thou shalt eat the herb of the field;

In the sweat of thy face shalt thou eat bread, till thou return unto the ground; for out of it wast thou taken: for dust thou art, and unto dust shalt thou return.

A CURSE AND A CONSEQUENCE

There are only two entities that are cursed in this narrative. In Moses we read: "And I, the Lord God, said unto the serpent: Because thou hast done this *thou shalt be cursed* above all cattle, and above every beast of the field; upon thy belly shalt thou go, and dust shalt thou eat all the days of thy life; And I will put enmity between thee and the woman, between thy seed and her seed; and he shall bruise thy head, and thou shalt bruise his heel" (Moses 4:20–21, emphasis added).

The imagery of the serpent (Satan) under the heel of the seed of the woman symbolically represents Christ's victory over death. Christ's "heel is bruised," referring to the Atonement, Crucifixion, and death. But the serpent's (Satan's) head will be crushed through Christ's resurrection.[1] Because of His resurrection, we will overcome the sting and bruising of death.

The second curse we read of is in Genesis 3:17, which clearly states that the *land* (the only true innocent in this narrative) is cursed. But the curse was pronounced for Adam's—and by extension, Eve's—sake. It would no longer be easy to get food and sustenance from the ground. Whereas in Eden food was at their fingertips, out in the world Adam and Eve would now be required to struggle, reaping the value of hard work and self-sufficiency, along with the harvest.

And then there is the matter of *consequences*. Eve's consequences, listed in verse 16 of Genesis 3, include:

1. Sorrow and conception will be multiplied.[2]
2. In sorrow, she will bring forth children.
3. Her desire shall be to her husband, and he shall rule over her.

SORROW AND CONCEPTION MULTIPLIED

Eve's act was a necessary transgression, decreed by God, as a doorway to eternal life.[3] Eve's initiative of partaking of the fruit allowed posterity for both Adam and Eve; and for that posterity the opportunity to grow, develop, and progress toward becoming like our Heavenly parents. It opened the door to pain and sorrow, but also for joy and progression. Without Adam and Eve's choices, they never would have had children[4]—clearly one of Elohim's commandments.[5]

Christian traditional interpretations draw the conclusion that "sorrow and conception multiplied" refers to the *physical* enlargement of the woman and the sorrow of bringing forth children was associated with the pain of childbirth. And, we know how the third consequence has been interpreted.

A careful study of the Hebrew words better illuminates these conditions, rendering all three of the consequences quite differently. Careful and calculated words were chosen by the scriptural author to represent both Adam and Eve's respective "suffering."[6]

Hugh Nibley, a Latter-day Saint scholar, noticed that the Hebrew word used in the Septuagint[7] for *multiply* is *plethynomai*, which "does not mean to add or increase but to repeat over and over again. . . . Both the conception and the labor of Eve will be multiple; [meaning that] she will have many children."[8] As we are to find joy in our posterity this is, of course, a good thing. When the Hebrew word *arbah* is used in the Abrahamic covenant,[9] it means "I will make you great."

God did not curse Eve or her daughters with physical enlargement during pregnancy because of her choice. Her *consequence* is tied to the natural order that her body will now be subject to.

Multiple children will make Eve great.

IN SORROW BRINGING FORTH CHILDREN

The Hebrew word used for sorrow is *atsav*. It means to toil, to do something hard, to labor anxiously. It is easy to conjure this mental image as it relates to childbirth. The root meaning, therefore, does not mean "to be sorry," but to *have a hard time.*

This identical word is used for the conditions and consequences of both Adam *and* Eve; yet it is puzzling that the translations do not reflect this. Both Adam and Eve must sorrow and labor to bring forth life: for Eve, through the bodies of the spirits waiting their turn on earth, and for Adam, so that the earth may bring forth life. Both will labor—with sweat and tears.[10]

Side by side, they are bound together in covenants, choices, and love. Mother Eve is bound to Father Adam, as she didn't want to leave him behind. He is also bound to her "because [he] hast hearkened unto [his] wife and, hast eaten of the fruit." He was willing to follow her, suffer for her, and suffer *with* her.[11]

DESIRE TO THY HUSBAND

The Hebrew word in Genesis 3:16 that is translated as *desire* is often culturally viewed as a master and slave, a "doer" and/or "helper," much in the context of a wife handing her husband the wrench as he does the "real" work. But the Hebrew word is *teshuqah* (tesh-oo-kaw), which is more accurately translated as "stretching out after" or "longing."[12]

There are many differing views and scholarly debates as to what God meant when he explained to Eve that her desire would be to her husband. The verbiage suggests that this longing is to please and be at one with Adam. In any culture, a woman desires to be treated like a queen by her husband and to know that she has value in the relationship, that he only has eyes for her.[13] In American and other cultures, a woman deserves to be an equal partner in a relationship. Perhaps this is one of the consequences Heavenly Father informs her of—a woman's longing for equality, and an escape from a historical and cultural tendency of some men seeking power and dominance over women, and (in some not-so-ancient cultures) treating them as property.

RULE OVER VERSUS RULE WITH

There have also been many challenges to the definition of the phrase *rule over*. Elder Bruce C. Hafen, in an article written with his wife, Marie, feels the correct interpretation should be *rule with*: "The concept of interdependent, equal partners is well-grounded in the doctrine of the restored gospel. Eve was Adam's 'help meet.'[14] The original Hebrew for 'meet' means that Eve was adequate for, or equal to, Adam. She wasn't his servant or his subordinate. . . . The Hebrew for help in 'help meet' is *ezer*, a term meaning that Eve drew on heavenly powers when she supplied their marriage with the spiritual instincts uniquely available to women as a gender gift."[15]

The phrase that has been translated as "he shall rule over thee" in English conveys a very different meaning in Hebrew. The Hafens clarify the subtext of our current English translation, as well as the Hebrew:

> Genesis 3:16 states that Adam is to "rule over" Eve, but this doesn't make Adam a dictator. A ruler can be a measuring tool that sets standards. Then Adam would live so that others may measure the rightness of their conduct by watching his. *Being a ruler is not so much a privilege of power as an obligation to practice what a man preaches.* Also, over in "rule over" uses the Hebrew *bet*, which means ruling with, not ruling over. If a man does exercise "dominion . . . in any degree of unrighteousness" (Doctrine and Covenants 121:37), God terminates that man's authority.[16]

A common mistake with readers of the Genesis account is in treating "desire" and "rule" as a *prescriptive* model rather than a *descriptive* one.[17] The imperfect translation took on an unintended template for the husband and wife relationship.

The cause and effect statements of Elohim concerning Adam and Eve, respectively, were not meant to be interpreted as curses *or* commandments, but rather as a tutorial on the upcoming effects of the mortality they have chosen. Elohim teaches Adam and Eve that when they fell, they took the earth with them. In the fallen state, nature will no longer automatically provide them with necessities of life, as it did so freely in the Garden of Eden.

And considering the real and present dangers of their new fallen world, perhaps the phrase "thy desire shall be to thy husband" indicates that, in her state of pregnancies, and in her role as main caregiver of children, Eve will desire and need her husband to "rule over" her—and their offspring—in a protective role, rather than a domineering "bossy-pants" type of head of household.

Even if the traditional, cultural interpretation was correct, to a loving Heavenly Father as well as in a happy and harmonious marriage, few would equate this "ruling over" as likening to that of a king over his subjects. It should be viewed as a righteous husband providing for, shielding, protecting, and *strengthening* his wife. His stewardship is to aid her in her duty, to bring forth and teach the next generation to live uprightly, righteously dedicated to the true and living God.

An interesting sidenote is that in Romans 5:12, Paul places the responsibility of the Fall squarely on the shoulders of Adam, not Eve. This is no small matter. A study of the Adam and Eve allegory raises questions such as, if Adam was tempted first, did he not warn Eve? Was he just as responsible for Eve's actions as his own? The curses pronounced and consequences explained by Elohim are wise and calculated as Adam is now held responsible for taking care of and providing for his family by laboring in the field; and Eve will do something very difficult for her body, toiling to bring forth children.

THE ALLEGORICAL NARRATIVE

There is more than one Adam and Eve narrative available to us, each with distinct differences. Moses wrote Genesis in a poetic, allegorical style, taking the chronological aspect of a (very real) historical couple and incident as a symbolic lesson for men and women.

One important episode in the narratives, included in all versions, is that of clothing Adam and Eve after they have partaken of the fruit. Satan, of course, cares little when he blithely instructs them to use leaves as a covering. Elohim, on the other hand, is greatly concerned with their well-being and protection, collectively and individually. He does not abandon them nor send them out from the garden defenseless. So as we examine curses, consequences, and now compassion, this is a prime example of God assisting us, wanting more than anything for us to succeed, even when we desperately get in our own way. Jolene Edmunds Rockwood said, "The Lord provides them with clothing (shields of knowledge) to cover their nakedness (defenselessness). They can now defend themselves against evil. His final response is thus an act of compassion, not punishment."[18]

It is valuable to recognize the actions of both Adam and Eve echoing that of Jesus Christ. Adam leaves paradise—Eden—and a life of ease to *ensure* mankind, just as Christ leaves his Heaven to *save* mankind. Eve, in order to bring new life into the world, must descend into the "valley of the shadow of death"[19] in childbirth, just as Christ descended below all things to offer eternal life to humanity. (She and her daughters come the closest to understanding the depth of pain Christ underwent in the Garden of Gethsemane.) Adam, Eve, and Christ were all willing to die so that mankind could live.

ENDNOTES

1. Corinthians 15:25–26
2. See also Moses 4:22.
3. Dallin H. Oaks, "The Great Plan of Happiness," *Ensign*, November 1993.
4. Moses 5:11; 2 Nephi 2:22–25
5. Genesis 1:28
6. "Apparently we have here a play upon words with reference to *es* [= tree]: it was with respect to *es* that the man and woman sinned, and it was with *esebb* [= pain] and *issabbon* [= toil, suffering] that they were punished. The very fact that Scripture does not employ here the usual phrases found in connection with the suffering of childbirth proves that it was some specific intention that these words were selected" (Umberto Cassuto, *Adam to Noah*, 165). See also Jeffrey M. Bradshaw, "A Curse for the Serpent and Blessings for Adam and Eve," *Meridian Magazine*, February 19, 2010. latterdaysaintmag.com/article-1–409/.

7. "The Septuagint is the Old Greek version of the Bible. It includes translations of all the books found in the Hebrew (Old Testament) canon, and as such it is the first known Bible translation. It also includes the so-called apocryphal or deuterocanonical books, some translated from Hebrew originals and others originally composed in Greek" (bibleodyssey.com/passages/related-articles/what-is-the-septuagint.aspx).

8. Hugh Nibley, "Patriarchy and Matriarchy," Neal A. Maxwell institute for Religious Scholarship, accessed October 15, 2019, mi.byu.edu/. (See also Hugh Nibley, "Patriarchy and Matriarchy," *Old Testament and Related Studies*, vol. 1 in *The Collected Works of Hugh Nibley* [Salt Lake City: Deseret Book Company and Foundation for Ancient Research & Mormon Studies (FARMS)], 1986).

9. Genesis 17:2

10. Genesis 3:17; Moses 4:23

11. Genesis 3:17–19

12. Strong's Hebrew Concordance, word 8669, biblehub.com/hebrew/8669.htm.

13. The clearest example of this is in the Book of Mormon, Jacob 2 (see especially verse 35). The prophet Jacob is chastising the men for breaking the hearts of their wives as they broke marriage covenants. These women desired that their husbands would be faithful, not only to them but to their family.

14. Genesis 2:18

15. Bruce C. Hafen and Marie K. Hafen, "Crossing Thresholds and Becoming Equal Partners," The Church of Jesus Christ of Latter-day Saints, August 2007, churchofjesuschrist.org/study/liahona/2007/08/crossing-thresholds-and-becoming-equal-partners?lang=eng.

16. Ibid, emphasis added.

17. Jeffrey Bradshaw, "A Curse for the Serpent and Blessings for Adam and Eve," *LDS Magazine*, February 19, 2010, latterdaysaintmag.com/article-1–409/.

18. Jolene Edmunds Rockwood, "The Redemption of Eve," in *Sisters in Spirit: Mormon Women in Historical and Cultural Perspective*, ed. Maureen Ursenbach. Beecher and Lavina Fielding Anderson (Urbana, I: University of Illinois Press, 1992), 15.

19. Psalm 23:4

Chapter 3

SEPARATION AND REPARATION

*[There are] three important interrelated
principles of marriage: leaving, cleaving, and
becoming one.*[1]

—Matthew O. Richardson

COMMANDMENT TO CLEAVE

Since the beginning of creation, there has been a theme of separation: light from darkness, land from water, woman from
man, man (*'adam*/mankind) from God. And ever since that
separation, caused by the Fall, men and women, husbands and wives,
have struggled to return to that unity, that binding, that *one-ness*.
God gives mankind commandments and offers them covenants to
bring this unity back into existence, including, most important, the
eternal plan of the Atonement. But immediately, for the benefit of
Adam and Eve, Elohim offers a divine directive for Adam to *cleave*
to Eve, his wife.[2]

Cleaving comes from the Hebrew word *devakut*, which is derived
from the Hebrew root *davak,* meaning "to cling, to stick close to,
to follow." But it actually has a much more profound meaning than

that. In Genesis, it is related to *debek*, the word used for bodily joint, much like the way our skin adheres to our bones. In other words, we are to cleave to God,[3] to our covenants, and to our spouse[4] as tightly *as our skin cleaves to our bones.*[5]

This mending of what is broken, and a return to the unity and harmony that once existed in the Garden, is "the essence of eternal life."[6] Adam and Eve are to return to unity with each other and with God.

POWER STRUGGLES

In the natural course of mortality, we see a gravitational pull toward pride, selfishness, and grappling for power within the marital relationship. We see the evidence of this in one biblical scholar's interpretation of the biblical word translated as *desire.* According to John H. Sailhammer, this desire does not indicate physical or sexual attraction, but rather "a wish to 'overcome or defeat another.'"[7]

What began as a co-equal relationship and partnership in the garden has been turned away, resorting to the two—Adam and Eve, husband and wife—attempting to dominate each other. It becomes a contest of wills and power struggles. Victor P. Hamilton wrote, "The two who once reigned as one attempt to rule each other."[8] Unfortunately, rarely are participants in marriage exempt from pride and selfishness.

Small differences are magnified into great ones, "and to reinforce the tendency toward hierarchy, division, and the rule of the 'superior' over the perceived inferior. Any relationship in which one member 'rules' over the other seems to be associated more with the fallen state than with the redeemed state."[9]

A celestial relationship cannot and will not be one of inequality. The differences between men and women are meant to unify as one, complements of each other.

SYMBOLIC ASPECTS OF THE FALL

As we study the story of Adam and Eve and analyze what it means for men and women in our current society, it helps to study it in the context with which it was written and intended. Author Jolene

Edmunds Rockwood writes: "Internal textual evidence shows that the Genesis account of the creation, temptation, and fall of Adam and Eve is most appropriately viewed as a piece of Hebrew poetry rather than as a literal historical account. . . . It uses a great deal of imagery, symbolism, and multi-leveled meaning. As is characteristic of this literary form, the Genesis Eden account is a tightly woven, symmetrical unit in which the meaning of the story is conveyed through imagery and parallelism."[10]

Currently there are at least four versions of the allegory of Adam and Eve: Genesis, Moses, Abraham, and Latter-day Saint temples. The account of the Creation and Fall is heavily symbolic and figurative, and was never intended to be interpreted as purely historical. In The Church of Jesus Christ of Latter-day Saints' faith, this concept of symbolism has been consistently taught from the beginning of the Restoration.

The accounts depicted in these books differ from each other and from the account depicted in the temple. It would be advised to view the temple ceremony as a general portrayal, layered with complexity and meaning, and not an actual historical account of either the Creation or the Fall.[11] The purpose and intent of the temple ceremony is to present ideas and teach principles through symbols and figurative language.

Temple ceremonies are layered with meanings that are only unlocked with consistent attendance and a sincere and prayerful approach to a spiritual understanding. Not all answers and enlightenment are transferrable from patron to patron, as some interpretations are predicated on life experiences and spiritual maturity. Rockwood wrote, "The exact creation of the man and the woman—especially the rib story—and the mode of the fall (the serpent and the fruit) have been interpreted as symbols of a much more complex historical actuality. Spencer W. Kimball, as president of the church, stated that the rib story 'of course is figurative.' Brigham Young . . . maintained, as did Joseph Smith, Joseph Fielding Smith, and others, that Adam and Eve's bodies were engendered and born by natural sexual functioning and that they were placed in Eden as adult beings."[12]

In addition to the rib story,[13] other elements are also considered symbolic, including the tree, the fruit, and the serpent. In fact, Orson Pratt and Hugh Nibley have indicated that there was more than one being tempting and persuading Adam and Eve to defy God's commandments.[14] Erastus Snow taught that Adam and Eve brought mortality and decay into their bodies "through their partaking of the fruits of the earth."[15]

In the allegorical accounts that we have of our first parents, this process of the Fall is represented through symbols and imagery that were, in part, intended for us to place ourselves in their stead, as if we were Adam or Eve.

WHICH VERSION ARE WE TO BELIEVE?

The Genesis account (3:1–6) indicates that Adam and Eve were not separated during the serpent's tempting. Eve partook and then gave some of the fruit to "her husband with her." But 1 Timothy 2:13–14 implies that Adam and Eve were separated when she was tempted and partook. If Eve was alone, she did not have all of the facts and had to make a decision based on what she could discern at the time.

When offering the fruit to Adam, Eve explained the situation and choices with more wisdom and guidance to her husband than what had been afforded her. No deception or coercion seems to be present in the Timothy account of Eve presenting the fruit and alternatives to Adam, nor does he seem to hesitate or waver. They appear to have made a unified decision.

Doctrine and Covenants 29:40 reads, "Wherefore, it came to pass that the devil tempted Adam, and he partook of the forbidden fruit and transgressed the commandment, wherein he became subject to the will of the devil, because he yielded unto temptation." This either indicates that 1) Adam was tempted alone and he partook of the fruit, or 2) 'adam/mankind was used as a title referring to both of them, rather the name of the male, indicating the two were together and viewed as one unit.

Which version is correct? Were they separate or together? Did Satan tempt Adam first or Eve? In what order did any of this take place? In reality, it doesn't matter, as *all versions* are symbolic. Jolene Edmunds Rockwood said, "We can infer, consequently, that whatever action one would take, the other would take also."[16]

Just as the four Gospels in the New Testament present different viewpoints, different Adam and Eve narratives have singular viewpoints of the same story. Each view is meant to relate a unique lesson for our benefit.

ENDNOTES

1. churchofjesuschrist.org/study/ensign/2005/04/three-principles-of-marriage?lang=eng)
2. Genesis 2:24
3. Deuteronomy 11:22, 13:4, Joshua 23:8
4. Matthew 19:5
5. Parsons, John. "תוקבד—Devakut—Cleaving to the LORD." Hebrew4Christians, n.d. hebrew4christians.com/Meditations/Devakut/devakut.html. Parsons also writes, "In Jewish mystical tradition, devakut is considered as the highest mystical step on the spiritual ladder back to God" while emphasizing that Jesus Christ is the true "ladder" to God.
6. Lynn A. McKinlay, "Patriarchal Order of the Priesthood," in *Encyclopedia of Mormonism*, vol. 3 (New York, NY: Macmillan Pub. Co., 1999), 1067.
7. Frank E. Gaebelein and John H. Sailhamer, "Genesis," in *The Expositor's Bible Commentary* (Michigan: Zondervan, 1992), 58.
8. Victor P. Hamilton, in *The Book of Genesis: Chapters 1–17* (Grand Rapids, MI: Eerdmans, 1995), 202.
9. Jolene Edmunds Rockwood, "The Redemption of Eve," in *Sisters in Spirit: Mormon Women in Historical and Cultural Perspective*, ed. Maureen Ursenbach. Beecher and Lavina Fielding Anderson (Urbana, I: University of Illinois Press, 1992), 18.
10. Ibid.
11. Hyrum L. Andrus, in *God, Man and the Universe*, 2nd ed., vol. 1 (Salt Lake City, UT: Bookcraft, 1970), 333–34. This footnote only appears in the earlier editions.
12. Rockwood, 15. See also Spencer W. Kimball, "The Blessings and Responsibilities of Womanhood," The Church of Jesus Christ

of Latter-day Saints, ChurchofJesusChrist.org/ensign/1976/03/
the-blessings-and-responsibilities-of-womanhood?lang=eng,
accessed October 21, 2019.

13. Ibid.

14. Orson Pratt, *Journal of Discourses*, Nov. 22 1873, 16:318. See also
Hugh Nibley, "Patriarchy and Matriarchy," Neal A. Maxwell
institute for Religious Scholarship, mi.byu.edu/, accessed October 15, 2019.

15. Erastus Snow, "There Is a God—Communion With Him An
Inherent Craving of the Human Heart—Man in His Image—
Male and Female Created He Them—Spirit and Flesh—Mortal
and Immortal," *Journal of Discourses*, journalofdiscourses.
com/19/40, accessed October 21, 2019.

16. Rockwood, 15.

Chapter 4
THE ISSUE OF CULTURE

*Some Christians condemn Eve for her act,
concluding that she and her daughters are
somehow flawed by it. Not the Latter-day
Saints! Informed by revelation, we celebrate
Eve's act and honor her wisdom and courage
in the great episode called the Fall.[1]*

—Dallin H. Oaks

So much of who we are is molded by culture—ethnic, national, familial, religious. What is often mistaken for original thought is actually defined and sustained by years of cultural indoctrination. Having established that, God usually works within and uses culture as He brings to pass His plans.

Throughout time, some men have used scriptures to justify the mistreatment of women, not acknowledging women's worth or worthy contributions. Historically, women have suffered the most repression and humiliation during spiritually dark times and in cultures where the gospel of Jesus Christ is not correctly practiced, or when it is forgotten. It is no secret that the Adam and Eve narrative has greatly influenced the Judeo-Christian view of women.

This has been a cultural excuse for the evil and wicked denigration, submission, and oppression of women, and is not prescribed by our Heavenly Parents. The Bible does not teach that men or women are to be punished for Adam and Eve's choices in the garden. The biblical account merely demonstrates that all of their children (including us) are affected by that choice, along with the earth. There is no verdict of supremacy of either sex in Genesis.

Thankfully, we are not just a conglomeration of socialized patterns; or, as one scholar phrased it, "a collective programming of the mind."[2] And despite that some of our culture is also genetically coded, an inheritance handed down "unto the third and fourth generation,"[3] we have been endowed with free will, with intellect to examine and change our future for the good.

PIECES OF A GREATER WHOLE

When Joseph Smith restored the Church of Jesus Christ, everything was eventually organized line upon line. But, in the early days of the Church—mirroring and harmonizing with the presiding Christian culture of *that* day—men led and preached in the Church, while the women often served in more subtle ways, engaging in charitable organizations and causes. However, God was just getting started and, much in the same way women's worth was magnified in His parables, Jesus Christ had a plan for the Church and for the men and women in it.

One concept that confuses many people, including Church members, is that this "line upon line" is not necessarily linear. The revelations that introduced correct principles of baptism, temple ordinances, the Word of Wisdom, and so on mostly came about because the leaders had questions, which they inquired about in prayer. In the early days of doctrinal restoration, the operation of the Church was not a clearly defined staircase or ladder where you could see where you're going and what lay at the end.

For instance, in 1842 a group of inspired Latter-day Saint women wanted to create a charitable organization (once again, in harmony with the culture of the day) initially with the idea to aid and serve the men who were working on the temple. When the women presented this idea (which later became known as the Relief Society) to Joseph Smith, this early prophet, inspired by the Spirit, sought to amplify an already good idea into something better. The prophet "would organize the women 'in the Order of the Priesthood after the pattern of the church.'"[4] By organizing it in the priesthood, he raised the cultural standing of the Latter-day Saint women of his day. "It was unlike other women's societies of the day because it was established by a prophet who acted with priesthood authority to give women authority, sacred responsibilities, and official positions within the structure of the Church, not apart from it. The women were organized, as Apostle John Taylor remarked at the founding meeting, 'according to the law of Heaven.'"[5]

So, in a given society and a time where men were culturally expected to take responsibility for the physical *and* spiritual welfare of women, Joseph Smith taught that women and men were responsible for their own sins. This was revolutionary in that day and age.

The battle is often distinguishing between culture, policy, and doctrine. Jesus Christ restored the doctrine, knowing that living it would change the culture.

LOOKING THROUGH THE PROPER LENS

One of the temptations is to look at ancient or historical events and scriptures through the lens of current time, demographics, and belief systems. Some become perplexed and even heated at directives and choices made by individuals living in an entirely different time period and set of circumstances. Society often attempts to whitewash history, wanting to forget that current culture and more came out of the past, including the good, the bad, and the ugly.

It must be remembered that context is king; that historical and cultural perspectives must be taken into account for greater and clearer understanding. People are not, and never were, perfect. Societal progress, including Latter-day Saint traditions, isn't perfect, but it helps to understand why things happened in the culture of that time period.

We don't have to agree with decisions and choices made at that time. We just need to understand the context in which they were made.

This is often done with scripture. A European-based culture took a repeatedly translated scripture (the Bible) and covered it with a heavy film to view it through. The original Hebrew roots and culture that the biblical scripture was originally dictated into is often misunderstood or ignored. Latter-day Saints already recognize that belief in the Bible is predicated upon the correctness of its translation.[6]

The narrative of Adam and Eve is no exception. Much of mainstream Christianity, from the earliest of times, has superimposed cultural views of women (and the role of a wife) onto the account, interpreting biblical consequences as it could fit into already established ideas, lifestyle, and stereotypes. The history of Adam and Eve is as much shaped and created by past—and contemporary—culture as current culture has been shaped by varied theological interpretations.

THE IMPORTANCE OF A CORRECT VIEW OF THE FALL

Mary Jane Woodger stated:

> By the time rabbis appeared as a distinct group in the second century, some of them saw the woman's role as God's punishment for Eve's transgression. Because Eve's disobedience caused not only her own death but also the demise of every other mortal (Ben Sira 25.24), she became the "fundamental character and identity of all women . . . through Eve's words and actions, the true nature of women was revealed." Most thought her nature was passed down to every daughter and included being "disobedient, guileless, weak-willed, prone to temptation and evil, disloyal, untrustworthy, deceitful, seductive, and motivated in their thoughts and behavior purely by self-interest."[7]

The Genesis account of Adam and Eve has so much cultural layering because the bottom line is we—that is, humans—are afraid. We are afraid of change, of finding out this neat and ordered world we think "we've" created isn't actually what God intends for us.

"The incorrect idea in Christian history that wives should be dependent began with the false premise that the Fall of Adam and Eve was a tragic mistake and that Eve was the primary culprit," Bruce and Marie Hafen wrote. "Thus women's traditional submission to men was considered a fair punishment for Eve's sin."[8] Through most of history Eve has been blamed for everything that could possibly go wrong. But as we strip away biases and cultural interpretations that have been passed down from generation to generation and look at what the original Hebrew text actually says, we will find that the account has very little of what Judeo-Christian cultures claim.

Societies' perception of Eve greatly influences how her daughters are treated and has a huge impact on how our own daughters' lives will unfold. Many traditions hold that, since Eve was created second, she is somehow a second-class citizen, that "she was an appendage to Adam, that she was somehow inferior to Adam, that being derivative of Adam and not derivative of God, that she was two steps away from divinity, not one step as Adam was."[9] As we discussed in the previous chapter, the idea of Eve being created from Adam's rib is merely symbolic and not literal.

CHOOSE CORRECT TRADITIONS

We live in a fallen world. God works within a current and given culture. He uses revelations, inspirations, and experiences to aid all of us in our eternal growth and progression.

An example of this would be revelation on the Word of Wisdom.[10] When it was first released it was a suggestion "sent by greeting, not by commandment or restraint."[11] It was given so that even the weakest of Saints could live by it. Working within the traditions of tobacco, tea, and coffee, the Lord introduced what would later become a commandment, giving Saints time to wrap their heads around a new way of life. But eventually, all Saints and disciples must choose the Lord's culture over their own: "The traditions or culture or way of life of a people inevitably include some practices that must be changed by those who wish to qualify for God's choicest blessings."[12]

As we continue to discuss the Adam and Eve narrative and all that entails, we need to be careful when modeling our family or society after our perceptions of Old Testament customs. It contains great counsel on universal gospel principles but is also coming from a very different, very rigid way of life. We learn from and model the lessons, not the traditions.

With that in mind, working within a culture does not equate to condoning it. God would rather draw us into the light than try to drive us out from the darkness.

BASTARDIZED EARLY DOCTRINE AND A SLOWLY SWINGING PENDULUM

Early church fathers used the story of Adam and Eve to define and defend the emerging Catholic doctrine and theology, thus creating a stronghold on the new culture within the early church; that of moving shared power away from women and into the hands of men (another consequence of the Dark Ages).

Rockwood wrote, "One obvious doctrinal connection with Eve was the origin of sin and evil in the world. Catholic explorations echoed much of the apocryphal and pseudepigraphical literature already in existence.[13] Irenaeus (died c. A.D. 200) wrote that evil and death entered the world through Eve, who then led the innocent Adam into sin, hardly an original observation.[14] This view of Eve, and thus of all women, as inherently seductive and weak-willed was important in ascribing to Eve sole responsibility for sin in the world."[15]

History continued to shape and reshape the story of Adam and Eve. The medieval period celebrated virginity as "the highest ideal of Christian life."[16] Martin Luther sparked the Protestant Reformation and preached that sin was characteristic of both men *and* women (Adam and Eve). And then with the nineteenth century suffrage movement[17] society began viewing the Fall with a new feministic lens.[18]

Even the early days of The Church of Jesus Christ of Latter-day Saints was not immune to interpreting the Adam and Eve story to support long established views and issues. George Q. Cannon taught in 1869 that polygamy would "redeem woman from the effects of [Eve's] curse." Brigham Young taught the doctrine of premortal polygyny, asserting that Eve was just one of Adam's wives.[19] It was also common for early General Authorities to cite 1 Timothy 2:14 to support the view that Eve was deceived by the serpent, so her subjection to Adam (and by extension all women to men) was a justified consequence.[20] This cultural trend has waned considerably, and we rarely hear a General Authority even suggesting such an interpretation. Instead, through continuing revelation, we take note—especially through clarifications in the temple ceremony—that both Adam and Eve made a conscious choice of leaving the garden in order to progress and bring life into the world.

The cultural underpinnings of early Latter-day Saint women sparked the hope of eventually achieving future equality with men as we read in this 1889 essay by Ruby Lamont:

> Since the days of Eve her daughters have lived under the curse of social inferiority to her brother man. In this generation the irksomeness of this condition has been displayed by the woman's movement for equal rights. This movement has met with slurs and opposition at every step, just as every truth has always been opposed by its adversary. . . . God, who made us all, and who is no respecter of persons, intended that woman should in every way be equal to man in dignity; but He also knew the station in which she would be placed while on earth, that her child-bearing and child-rearing sphere would curtail other aspirations, which man would have the opportunity to follow. Of the two He knew that the former would be of the greater importance to the world, and therefore in the guise of a curse, bestowed upon her the blessing to be subject to man, that she might the better fulfill her mission. . . . To me it seems like one of the latter day signs, that women are becoming restless beneath their oppressed situation. The world's record will soon be finished. . . . And when the millennium shall set in, and the curse be removed . . . I write with confidence, for I firmly believe that *our Heavenly Father loves his daughters just as well as he loves His sons, and that He does not desire the glorification of one at the sacrifice of the happiness of the other.*"[21]

It is important to pause here and reiterate that as we view past and historical events, especially within the restored Church of Jesus Christ's history, we need to ask questions as they pertain to the context within culture and norms of that time period, rather than viewing them through a twenty-first century lens. Culturally speaking, woman is slowly coming to her own, "exercising her rights and her privileges as a sanctified investiture which none shall dare profane."²²

CONTINUING REVELATION

Today both men and women serve side by side in The Church of Jesus Christ of Latter-day Saints. Both genders serve full-time proselytizing missions, officiate in the Church's temples, and lead and preach sermons in organizations on both the local and worldwide levels of the Church. Women are full participants in priesthood councils and are considered ministers with their male counterparts.²³

The Brethren of the Church, while always very respectful toward women, continue to clarify doctrine pertaining to the roles of women. Just a few examples include:

- New insights in the temple ceremony that help to explain the choices made by both Adam and Eve.
- The change in female missionary ages.
- Women serving in missionary leadership positions.
- More women encouraged to participate and vocalize as equals in local and general leadership councils.
- The simple addition of women praying in general conference.

These are just a few examples of these bold clarifications and expanding roles of women in the Church, with certainty of more to follow. However, as women we must continue to be cautious, careful, and vigilant. Just when we think we've reached an era of enlightenment concerning our worth and roles, false concepts and ideas begin to surface, emanating from both the outside world and inside the gates. Unfortunately, it's women who seem to be the hardest on each other, one group callously suggesting a lack faith in the other or other groups labeling fellow sisters as closed-minded or unenlightened.

As Latter-day Saints, especially as women, we must band together as sisters in the gospel, with an eagerness to, as M. Russell Ballard put it, "encourage, accept, understand, and love those who are struggling with their faith," especially when it comes to matters of the ever-evolving roles of women within the restored church of Jesus Christ. "We must never neglect any of our . . . sisters. We are all at different places on the path, and we need to minister to one another accordingly."[24] Only then can we countermand the effects of centuries of incorrect views of the Fall and of Mother Eve. We can change our culture, one heart at a time.

ENDNOTES

1. Dallin H. Oaks, "The Great Plan of Happiness," *Ensign*, November 1993, 73.
2. Geert H. Hofstede, in *Cultures and Organizations: Software of the Mind* (New York, NY: McGraw-Hill, 1991), 5.
3. Exodus 20:2–6
4. ChurchofJesusChrist.org/topics/joseph-smiths-teachings-about-priesthood-temple-and-women?lang=eng.
   Some accounts, such as Sarah M. Kimball's and Reynolds Cahoon's, remember Joseph Smith's statement as "under the priesthood after the pattern of the priesthood" and "according to the Order of God connected with the priesthood." Which actual phrase was used is not as important as the sentiment, the sense of what Joseph saw in the design, the organization, and function of the Relief Society. He envisioned it working as the other half of the Church: under the direction of and beside the priesthood, with a three-member presidency that had been established in the priesthood quorums.
   Sarah M. Kimball, "Early Relief Society Reminiscence," *Relief Society Record, 1880–1892*, Mar. 17, 1882.
   Sarah M. Kimball, "Auto-Biography," *Woman's Exponent* 12, no.7:51; Nauvoo Relief Society Minutes, Aug. 13, 1843, available at josephsmithpapers.org.
5. Joseph Smith's Teachings about Priesthood, Temple, and Women, ChurchofJesusChrist.org/topics/joseph-smiths-teachings-about-priesthood-temple-and-women?lang=eng.
6. Articles of Faith 1:8
7. Mary Jane Woodger, "Jesus Christ's Interactions With the Women of the New Testament," *Interpreter: A Journal of Latter-Day Saint*

29

Faith and Scholarship 18 (2016): 15–32. journal.interpreterfoundation.org/jesus-christs-interactions-with-the-women-of-the-new-testament/.

8. Bruce C. and Marie K, Hafen, "Crossing Thresholds and Becoming Equal Partners," *Ensign*, August 2007.

9. Valerie Hudson Cassler, "The Two Trees." FairMormon, 2010. fairmormon.org/conference/august-2010/the-two-trees.

10. Doctrine and Covenants 89

11. Doctrine and Covenants 89:2

12. Dallin H. Oaks, "Repentance and Change," The Church of Jesus Christ of Latter-day Saints, October 2003. ChurchofJesusChrist.org/general-conference/2003/10/repentance-and-change?lang=eng.

13. For instance, the Gnostic writing of the Gospel of Philip (Nag Hammadi Library) claims Cain was born of Eve and the serpent Satan.

14. Irenaeus, *Adversus Haereses* 3, 22, 4; 3, 23, 5; 4, Preface, 4; 4, 38, 1–4; 4, 39, 2; 5, 19, 1; 5, 23, 1; as used in Bernard P. Prusak, "Woman: Seductive Siren and Source of Sin?" in Ruether, *Religion and Sexism*, 100–101.

15. Jolene Edmunds Rockwood, "The Redemption of Eve," in *Sisters in Spirit: Mormon Women in Historical and Cultural Perspective*, ed. Maureen Ursenbach. Beecher and Lavina Fielding Anderson (Urbana, I: University of Illinois Press, 1992), 18.

16. Ibid.

17. Many people question why the Restoration needed to take place in the United States. Why not Brazil or Sweden or another country in Europe? God works within cultures and according to a people's readiness to receive something that even in that time was considered new and bold. The U.S. Constitution guarantees religious freedom. The United States as a country was founded upon religious principles, with the majority of people seeking refuge for religious freedom; it was a place theoretically unbound by man's whims and prejudices. While we have not had a perfect history, this has been and is an exceptional country.

18. Elizabeth Cady Stanton et al., *The Woman's Bible* (Seattle: Coalition Task Force on Women and Religion, 1974), 26–27.

19. Brigham Young. "Self Government-Mysteries-Etc.," *Journal of Discourses* 1:46–53, jod.mrm.org/1/46, accessed October 23, 2019.

20. See for instance Brigham Young, *Journal of Discourses* 6:145; Orson Pratt, 21:288–89; Wilford Woodruff, 23:125; George Q. Cannon, 26:188–89.

21. Ruby Lamont, "The Woman's Movement," *Woman's Exponent*, February 1, 1889, emphasis added.

22. James E Talmage, "The Eternity of Sex," *Young Woman's Journal*, October 1914.

23. "Joseph Smith's Teachings about Priesthood, Temple, and Women," The Church of Jesus Christ of Latter-day Saints, ChurchofJesusChrist.org/topics/joseph-smiths-teachings-about-priesthood-temple-and-women?lang=eng, accessed October 23, 2019.

24. M. Russell Ballard, "To Whom Shall We Go?" The Church of Jesus Christ of Latter-day Saints, churchofjesuschrist.org/study/general-conference/2016/10/to-whom-shall-we-go?lang=eng, accessed October 2016.

Chapter 5

HOW CHRIST VIEWED WOMEN

*The world's greatest champion of
woman and womanhood is Jesus Christ.*[1]

—James E. Talmage

AN OLD JEWISH NARRATIVE

The culture during and after Christ was a difficult one for the female population.[6] First-century attitudes toward women were not generally positive. Men were valued more than women, and some cultures, such as the Greek, were openly hostile to females. It was not unusual to expose newborn female children to the elements as a means of termination. Women had no voice and were at the whim of their fathers and husbands, who literally had power over their lives. Wives had no legal or civil rights and were rarely allowed to divorce their husbands for any reason; in addition they were not allowed to own property, nor have money of their own. All of this left the female gender in a very vulnerable position.

Jesus, having been raised in a faithful Jewish household, would have studied the Torah alongside His peers. We know from the four gospels that He was well versed in the scriptures and the current law.

In spite of all of this, we do not read in any of the gospels a single example of Jesus using the Adam and Eve story as a justification for gender roles or to place the charge of "original sin" on the woman's shoulders. He taught that consequences for sin lay within the individual and demonstrated respect for women and their contribution as disciples.

In fact, some of His closest associates and disciples were women, as they were welcomed and encouraged to participate fully in the gospel. For instance, by Jesus gently correcting Martha, reminding her that her sister Mary had "chosen that good part, which shall not be taken away from her,"[9] He expanded "dramatically the structured role of a righteous Jewish woman by enabling her to study the scriptures as a man would do."[10]

Jesus taught using familiar cultural customs during His mortal ministry, using well-known imagery of His day. God works with us and moves us forward, challenging what we think we understand today to help us progress and prepare for a future He has in mind for us. God does not change with the times; it is us who change, both within and despite our times. But just as Jesus was born into, raised, lived, and taught within His own unique culture, He actively brought to light those things that were often ignored or passed over, such as the divine role of women.

Examine His parables, for instance. He deftly switched back and forth between male and female subjects and examples, subtly emphasizing the equality and importance of both,[2] including that of using metaphors that draw from "the feminine face of God."[3]

The first recorded scriptural witnesses of Christ's divine Messiahship have been women. The woman of Samaria testified and bore witness that Christ was the Messiah.[4] Mary Magdalene was the first witness of the resurrected Christ.[5] He instructed Mary to return to the Apostles and relate to them that Jesus had ascended to His father. It was no coincidence that Jesus chose a woman to carry this most significant message. It was merely another example and witness of the profound love and respect He had for women.

Mark's narrative in the New Testament demonstrates Christ's unusual attitude toward women, especially in contrast to the culture of His day. Mark's account draws attention to the women present at the Crucifixion.[11] During that time the Jews forbad females as witnesses (at least as the Torah was interpreted at that time), yet here the women are. And as all the male disciples have fled, we would not have this account were it not for these women and their testimony. The fact that Mark has publicly recognized the women implies that "Jesus's death has opened new roles and responsibilities for women."[12]

THE RENTING OF THE VEIL

Also in this account we are shown the torn veil, the centurion (a gentile), and a woman. The culture of Christ's day restricted both Gentiles and women from full temple worship. Both had been "formally excluded from the symbolic presence of the Lord."[13] The rent veil symbolizes that access is now obtainable to everyone, not just the high priest. Julie Smith taught, "What was previously restricted—the divine presence, knowledge, and ministry—is now available to all:"[14] gentile, Jew, male, and female. "They can be symbolically invited into the presence of the Lord, where they can share God's knowledge and have a role in Jesus's ministry."[15]

Mark, and other gospel writers who share accounts of female disciples, recognized that Christ went against the traditional grain of the Jewish culture, of the *male* Jewish culture. These writers revealed that Christ was a rebel and cultural activist, placing women far above what His upbringing would have dictated. Christ saw women for who they were, and sees them now for who they are: equal in the sight of God, bearing testimony and witness for Him, some serving in public ministries, but accepting and consecrating those ministries that are private and personal as well.

Bonnie Thurston said, "Jesus not only raised the status of women but put them on equal spiritual footing with men."[16] Mary Jane Woodger added:

> In this particular story [of Mary and Martha], Mary's actions are different than her sister's. She was daring since we have no examples from Palestine of a male teacher instructing women. In this account,

Mary acts like a male disciple, sitting at Jesus's feet to be taught . . . the relationship between Jesus and Mary "breached convention, for at that time women were not usually able to discuss the gospel with men." This story can be viewed as the basis of the "changed status of women thanks to Jesus and his teachings," showing that women could be independent disciples who were fully accepted by Christ "without male intermediaries such as fathers, brothers or husbands."[17]

In addition to this narrative we have the account of this same Mary anointing the Savior in preparation for his burial,[18] with expensive spikenard, the amount equivalent to a year's wages.[19] This spiritually-in-tune woman openly and publicly expressed that she grasped the full measure of Christ's teachings that He would suffer and die and that the time was imminent. This was not just an act of adoration and worship but also "suggestive of definite and solemn purpose on Mary's part."[20]

Mary's actions emanated from a place of great affection and love. Surely these feelings did not grow from Jesus maintaining the status quo of the cultural dogma of the day. His behavior had such an impact on women—as well as men—as He challenged each individual to examine the self and embrace and "love your neighbor as yourself."[21]

CHRIST PUBLICLY RECOGNIZED THE VALUE OF WOMEN

The Jewish culture did not allow for men to address women in public. And yet Jesus speaks openly with such women as the widow of Nain and brings her son back to life.[22] When He heals a crippled woman, Christ is called out for it by a Jewish synagogue leader. In response, Jesus refers to this woman as a "daughter of Abraham."[23] Prior to this time, only men were called "sons of Abraham" to signify their covenants that bound them to God. By using an expression that had earlier been reserved only for men, Christ is recognizing her heritage, clearly calling attention to her equal status as a woman of the covenant.

He even enters into a dialogue with a Samaritan woman. In surprise, she asks, "How is it that thou, being a Jew, askest drink of me, which am a woman of Samaria?"[24] She is confused that He would even talk with a Samaritan, let alone a Samaritan *woman*. Even His own Apostles were surprised, hesitantly questioning their master, "Why talkest thou with *her*?"[25]

He not only steps out of the Jewish cultural belief (of that time) that a woman was not trustworthy, but even allows a *foreign* woman to witness of him; and because of this, "many of the Samaritans of that city believed on him *for the saying of the woman, which testified*" (emphasis added).

We read of a woman with the issue of blood healed by the mere touching of Christ's robes.[26] According to the Mosaic law, she was unclean because of her bleeding[27] (and just by touching His robe He is also rendered unclean). When you add in the Jewish sub-culture of that day that believed that any illness was seen as a consequence of sin, her perpetual bleeding made her continually unclean, marginalized, and an outcast from society. The subculture had twisted the law, creating abandonment for this woman and intense loneliness. Instead of humiliating her, Christ's reaction was one of compassion.[28] He announced her clean and told her to go in peace.[29]

GOD IS THE SAME YESTERDAY, TODAY, AND TOMORROW[30]

While Christ used the culture He was born into to teach and instruct, He did not allow it to be a crutch or an excuse for holding onto that which did not, and does not, serve society or culture as a whole. His aim was to lead His followers, students, and disciples up and out of the cloudy and bastardized culture that had existed for centuries. He was able to introduce them to a higher way of living.

To study Christ's life is to see that He viewed all human beings—male, female, bond, free—as equals, and sin as the only de-equalizing force.

Scriptural evidence suggests that Christ felt a special kinship with women, especially mothers, and vice versa. Mothers descend dangerously close to death to bring forth mortal life, just as Christ did to bring forth spiritual life.

Jeffrey R. Holland stated, "Maternal love *has* to be divine. There is no other explanation for it. What mothers do is an essential element of Christ's work."[31]

Elder Matthew Cowley boldly declared, "Good women in our lives 'belong to the great sorority of saviorhood . . . born with an inherent right, an inherent authority to be the saviors of human souls."[32]

ENDNOTES

1. James Edward Talmage, in *Jesus the Christ; a Study of the Messiah and His Mission According to Holy Scriptures Both Ancient and Modern* (Salt Lake City, UT: Deseret Book, 1970).
2. See, for instance, the parable of the lost coin, Luke 15:8–10; the widow and the unjust judge, Luke 20:1–8; the woman and the leavened meal, Luke 13:20–21 and Matthew 13:33; the ten virgins, Matthew 25:1–13; women grinding at the mill, Matthew 24:41 and Luke 17:35.
3. Karen Jo Torjesen, *When Women Were Priests: Women's Leadership in the Early Church and the Scandal of Their Subordination in the Rise of Christianity* (New York, NY: HarperOne, 2011), 259. See also Deuteronomy 32:11–12, 18; Job 38:8; Hosea 13:8; Isaiah 46:3–4, 49:15; Matthew 23:37.
4. John 4:22–26
5. John 20:1–2
6. See, for instance, Ben Witherington, *Women in the Ministry of Jesus: a Study of Jesus' Attitudes to Women and Their Roles as Reflected in His Earthly Life* (Cambridge: Cambridge University Press, 2001).
7. The Midrash, Mishna, and Talmud are Old Testament commentaries and interpretations of the Torah written by rabbis and scribes.
8. Luke 8:1–3
9. Luke 10:38–42
10. Jolene Edmunds Rockwood, "The Redemption of Eve," in *Sisters in Spirit: Mormon Women in Historical and Cultural Perspective*, ed. Maureen Ursenbach. Beecher and Lavina Fielding Anderson (Urbana, I: University of Illinois Press, 1992), 3–29.

11. Mark 15:40–41
12. Julie M. Smith, "Narrative Atonement Theology in the Gospel of Mark." *BYU Studies*, 2015, 40.
13. Smith, 41.
14. Ibid., 36.
15. Ibid., 41.
16. Bonnie Thurston, "Questions and Commentary," *Women in the New Testament* (New York: Crossroads Publishing, 1998), 160.
17. Mary Jane Woodger, "Jesus Christ's Interactions with the Women of the New Testament." The Interpreter Foundation, journal. interpreterfoundation.org/jesus-christs-interactions-with-the-women-of-the-new-testament/, accessed August 27, 2019.
18. Mark 14:8
19. Mark 14:5
20. Talmage
21. Matthew 22:37–40
22. Luke 7:11–17
23. Luke 13:16
24. John 4:9
25. John 4:27, emphasis added
26. Mark 5:26
27. Leviticus 15: 25–30
28. See other examples, such as allowing the woman to anoint Him (Luke 8:39–44), and showing compassion on the woman caught in adultery (John 8:3–11).
29. Luke 8:43–48
30. Mormon 9:9
31. Jeffrey R. Holland, "Behold Thy Mother," The Church of Jesus Christ of Latter-day Saints, October 2015, ChurchofJesusChrist. org/general-conference/2015/10/behold-thy-mother?lang=eng.
32. Matthew Cowley, *Matthew Cowley Speaks: Discourses of Elder Matthew Cowley of the Quorum of the Twelve of the Church of Jesus Christ of Latter-Day Saints* (Salt Lake City, UT: Deseret Book, 1976), 76.

Chapter 6

TITLES VERSUS NAMES

These references are actually a recognition of His divinity and holiness—He is the Son of Man of Holiness, God the Father.[1]

—D. Todd Christofferson

There is none other name given under heaven, save it be this Jesus Christ, whereby man can be saved.

—2 Nephi 25:20

It seems that much of what confuses people about gender roles can be boiled down to labels: the titles, names, and mantles that are often gender driven. There is a difference between a *name* and a *title*. The scriptures and the Latter-day Saint temple ceremony distinguish between the two, and a large part of personal revelation is tied to understanding our relationship to those specific titles and names. Below are just a few.

ELOHIM

Elohim is the name *and* title used for the highest deity. This name connotes plurality, such as in Genesis 1:26–27: "And God said, Let us

41

make man in *our* image, after *our* likeness: and let them have dominion over the fish of the sea, and over the fowl of the air, and over the cattle, and over all the earth, and over every creeping thing that creepeth upon the earth. So God created man in his own image, in the image of God created he him; male and female created he them" (emphasis added).

We can relate the plural title *Elohim* much as we do to married couples or partners, like the Smiths or the Joneses. But as perfect partners, they would act as one, working together as the perfect team—as one flesh. When we speak of God the Father, we of course are referring to a single entity, but we can also see *God* as a title of two individual parents working in perfect harmony for the good of their children.

GOD

God is a title and a mantle. According to Latter-day Saint theology, any individual, through making and keeping sacred covenants and living a moral and righteous life, having kept all of the requirements set forth by our Heavenly Father, may one day become a god.[2] However, *God* as a title and a mantle can cover *more than one person at a time.*

In 2 Nephi 31:21 we read, "The Father, and of the Son, and of the Holy Ghost, which is *one God*"[3] (emphasis added). This verse highlights a critical difference between the doctrine of The Church of Jesus Christ of Latter-day Saints and mainstream Christian theology. Such references to Father and Son, or Father, Son, and Holy Ghost are about unity in purpose rather than as unity as a single entity.

According to Erastus Snow, *God* is not a single male personage but rather both Heavenly Father *and* Heavenly Mother:

"What," says one, "do you mean we should understand that Deity consists of man and woman?" Most certainly I do. If I believe anything that God has ever said about himself, and anything pertaining to the creation and organization of man upon the earth, I must believe that Deity consists of man and woman. Now this is simplifying it down to our understanding, and the great Christian world will be ready to open their mouths and cry, "Blasphemy! Sacrilege!" Open wide their eyes and wide their mouths in the utmost astonishment. What! God a man and woman?[4]

There can be no *God* except he is composed of the man and woman united, and there is not in all the eternities that exist, nor ever will be, a *God* in any other way.[5]

LORD (ALL CAPITAL LETTERS)

Out of strong reverence, Jews refused to say the name of Jehovah, instead substituting *Adonai*, a Hebrew *title* that means "Lord" or "My Lord." King James translators, following the same pattern, substituted the *name* of Jehovah with the English *title* LORD, all capital letters.[6]

Lord or lord (lowercase)

In the King James Version of the Bible, *Lord* or *lord* is a *title* referring to God, king, husband, prophet, and so on, but never Jehovah.[7] Just as *God*, the title *Lord* can also be used as a title or a mantle that covers more than one person at a time, such as in a presidency. We speak of decisions from "the board" or "a presidency," numerically plural, but singular in purpose.

ADAM (NAME)

Moses records that there have been many Adams: "And the first man of all men have I called Adam, which is many."[8]

'adam (LOWERCASE A)

The term *'adam* is a title and is considered a plural word that represents both the man *and* the woman. Both Adam and Eve are called *'adam*: "Male and female created he them; and blessed them, *and called their name Adam.*"[9]

Adam can be a proper noun (as in the book of Moses), as well as a collective noun as in "humankind," or both male and female. Adam becomes the perfect example of how a word can switch from singular to plural, from proper name to title in a single verse or sentence, based upon the context.

Spencer W. Kimball taught this eloquently (his own commentaries are bracketed):

"And I, God, blessed them [Man here is always in the plural. It was plural from the beginning.] and said unto them: Be fruitful, and multiply, and replenish the earth, and subdue it, and have dominion over [it]." (Moses 2:27–28.)

And the scripture says, "And I, God said unto mine Only Begotten, which was with me from the beginning: Let us make man [not a separate man, but a complete man, which is husband and wife] in our image, after our likeness; and it was so." (Moses 2:26.) What a beautiful partnership! Adam and Eve were married for eternity by the Lord. Such a marriage extends beyond the grave. All peoples should call for this kind of marriage. . . .

"Male and female created he them; and blessed them, and called their name Adam [Mr. and Mrs. Adam, I suppose, or Brother and Sister Adam], in the day when they were created." (Genesis 5:1–2.)"[10]

EVE[11]

Adam called the earth's first female *ishshah,* which "represented as intimate and sacred beyond that between child and parents."[12] It means woman—or more literally, "man-ess." The Greek word is *Heua* (yoo'-ah) or "the first woman."[13]

It is important to clarify here that *Adam did not name Eve.* In Moses 1:34 and 4:26 we read that *Adam* and *Eve* were titles that God gave to His first man and woman of any newly created worlds. When Adam "calls" the woman Eve he is merely referring to a previously known title that had been given by God.[14] In classical Hebrew the name/title Eve is *awwāh*[15] (or *Havah*), meaning "living one," "source of life" or "life giver." *Hawwāh* is also closely related to another Hebrew word, *Hāyâ:* "alive" or "living." Both words have the same semitic root *hyw* which means "to live."[16]

She—the first woman and Adam's help meet—is now called "Life, the mother of all living,"[17] and is a divine title of great honor.[18] It is significant to note that Eve was known as the "mother of all living" *before* she had children.

Adam recognized Eve as life!

With the different translations and interpretations of the Adam and Eve narrative, some report Adam recognizing Eve's name before partaking of the fruit. Others, such as Genesis 3:17–20, seem a bit more abrupt. Immediately following Elohim's review of impending consequences for disobedience, Adam turns to Eve and refers to her title. But Shira Halevi,[19] a noted female rabbi and Jewish scholar, shares a unique interpretation of the Hebrew text of these Genesis verses.

The traditional Masoretic translation reads:

> Thorns
> and thistles
> will she (earth) sprout for you
> and you will eat grain
> of the plowed field

Halevi interprets it as:

> Awake! Arise!
> generation upon generation
> will she (Havah) [Eve] spring for you
> and you will enjoy the yield of her breast

This interpretation has a much more logical flow, making sense of Adam *reacting with delight,* despite Elohim's "sentencing." Adam joyfully calls Eve "Life!" as she will now bring forth children—"generation upon generation."

He also did not reference her in any possessive way, that she was somehow connected to him. In other words, he did not refer to her as his servant or his helpmeet. Adam recognized her "as a separate individual with a mission and talents and their oneness would come about by adding to each other."[20]

JESUS CHRIST

Jesus Christ is the most important name and title that exists, and if we strip everything down to what is truly essential, the only "name given under heaven whereby man can be saved in the kingdom of God."[21] Our united purpose and mission on this earth is to take upon us His name, make the same covenants, follow His example, think as He thought, and obey our Heavenly Father as He did His. Our time here is limited, but our direction is clear. Sometimes we tend to get tangled in the weeds, but if we look up and focus on what is really important, our path will be much smoother and clearer.

MAN OF HOLINESS

Enoch taught that in the language of Adam, Heavenly Father is called Man of Holiness.[22] It is another one of God the Father's names. Holiness is one of the chief characteristics of Jesus Christ and Heavenly Father. We are all to seek for holiness.

CHIEF

You've most likely heard the popular saying, "You can't have two chiefs!" However, when *chief* is a title that covers two partners, then, yes, technically you *can* have two chiefs. One example is when we will one day enter into the presence of the Lord. In a specific context, Lord is not just one person—Heavenly Father or Jesus Christ. Lord is two entities—*both* Heavenly Father *and* Jesus Christ. One will be the voice, but two will be the *chief.*

Names and titles play an integral role in our cultural identification as well as our relationship within a group or with another individual. Especially within The Church of Jesus Christ of Latter-day Saints, names and titles are not and cannot be taken lightly. Calling someone by their proper name and title becomes a recognition of their worth, mission, and sense of identity.

The gospel of Jesus Christ and its earthly kingdom are continually in a state of restoration, and part of this restoration will be to address the missing language within the restored Church of Jesus Christ. The masculine needs the feminine; the man needs the woman, and vice versa. The times are still unfolding where woman is finally emerging from the wilderness,[23] taking her place by the side of the man, with full title and equity.

ENDNOTES

1. (Todd Christofferson, "The Living Bread Which Came Down from Heaven," The Church of Jesus Christ of Latter-day Saints, October 2017, ChurchofJesusChrist.org/liahona/2017/11

/saturday-morning-session/the-living-bread-which-came-down-from-heaven?lang=eng#

2. This idea of mortals becoming gods did not originate with The Church of Jesus Christ of Latter-day Saints. The early church father Irenaeus, who died about A.D. 202, asserted that Jesus Christ "did, through His transcendent love, become what we are, that He might bring us to be what He is Himself."[12] Clement of Alexandria (ca. A.D. 150–215) wrote that "the Word of God became man, that thou mayest learn from man how man may become God."[13] Basil the Great (A.D. 330–379) also celebrated this prospect—not just "being made like to God," but "highest of all, the being made God." See ChurchofJesusChrist.org/topics/becoming-like-god?lang=eng.

3. Other references to the Father, Son, and Holy Ghost as one God include the Testimony of Three Witnesses, Mosiah 15:3–5, Alma 11:44, 3 Nephi 11:27, and Mormon 7:7.

4. Erastus Snow, "There Is a God—Communion With Him An Inherent Craving of the Human Heart-Man in His Image—Male and Female Created He Them—Spirit and Flesh-Mortal and Immortal," *Journal of Discourses*, vol. 19, March 1978, journalofdiscourses.com/19/40, accessed November 6, 2019. (This passage does not suggest God is both male and female but rather reiterates unity in marriage and the creation of our first parents, both male and female.)

5. Ibid., emphasis added.

6. See Keith H. Meservy, "LORD = Jehovah," The Church of Jesus Christ of Latter-day Saints, Churchofjesuschrist.org/study/ensign/2002/06/lord-equals-jehovah?lang=eng, accessed November 6, 2019.

7. Ibid.

8. Moses 1:33–34

9. Genesis 5:2, emphasis added. See also Hugh Nibley, "Patriarchy and Matriarchy," *Old Testament and Related Studies*, vol. 1 in *The Collected Works of Hugh Nibley* (Salt Lake City: Deseret Book Company and Foundation for Ancient Research & Mormon Studies [FARMS]), 1986.

10. Spencer W. Kimball, "The Blessings and Responsibilities of Womanhood," The Church of Jesus Christ of Latter-day Saints. ChurchofJesusChrist.org/ensign/1976/03/the-blessings-and-responsibilities-of-womanhood?lang=eng, accessed October 21, 2019.

11. See Strong, *Strong's Exhaustive Concordance*, Hebrew word 2332.

12. Eve in the Old Testament, International *Standard Bible Encyclopedia*, internationalstandardbible.com/E/eve-in-the-old-testament.html.

13. Strong's Greek Concordance, 2096, biblehub.com/greek/2096.htm.

14. It is also interesting to note that this is reminiscent of a "Near Eastern formula for titles given to goddesses." Dawn Hall Anderson, Marie Cornwall, and Jolene Edmunds Rockwood, "Eve's Role in the Creation and the Fall to Mortality," in *Women and the Power within: to See Life Steadily and See It Whole,* (Salt Lake City, UT: Deseret Book 1991), 49–62. See also Isaac M. Kikawada, "Two Notes on Eve," *Journal of Biblical Literature* 91 (1972):33–37.

15. thefreedictionary.com/Eves.. Also spelled *chawwah,* or *chavvah* (khav-vaw') See also Strong's Hebrew Concordance, 2332

16. thefreedictionary.com/_/roots.aspx?type=Semitic&root=hyw

17. It should be noted that this three element name—x of all the y—is an ancient formula used for personal names of honor. (See Kikawada, 33–37.)

18. Kikawada, 33–37. Adam also calls her *'ēm kol-hhay,* which is a title of honor for a great lady. See also Alfred Jones, *The Proper Names of the Old Testament Scriptures Expounded and Illustrated,* 120.

19. Shira Halevi, in *The Life Story of Adam and Havah: a New Targum of Genesis 1:26–5:5* (Aronson, 1997), 202.

20. Sherrie Johnson, *Man, Woman, and Deity,* (Salt Lake City, Utah: Bookcraft, 1991), 18.

21. 2 Nephi 31:21

22. Moses 6:57

"Enoch counseled us, 'Teach it unto your children, that all men, everywhere, must repent, or they can in nowise inherit the kingdom of God, for no unclean thing can dwell there, or dwell in his presence; for, in the language of Adam, Man of Holiness is his name, and the name of his Only Begotten is the Son of Man, even Jesus Christ.' As a boy, I wondered why in the New Testament Jesus is often referred to (and even refers to Himself) as the Son of Man when He is really the Son of God, but Enoch's statement makes it clear that these references are actually a recognition of His divinity and holiness—He is the Son of Man of Holiness, God the Father" (D. Todd Christofferson, "The Living Bread Which Came Down from Heaven," The Church of Jesus Christ of Latter-day Saints, October 2017, ChurchofJesusChrist.org/liahona/2017/11/saturday-morning-session/the-living-bread-which-came-down-from-heaven?lang=eng#note22–

23. Revelation 12:6

Chapter 7
WE ARE 'ADAM

The Book of the Generations
  begettings
  accounting
Of the couple, Adam
In the likeness of Divine Ones He shaped them
  male and female
    man and woman
He fashioned them
He blessed them and called their name Adam
                    red/blood/earth/dust
                    Humanity[1]
            —The Life Story of Adam and Havah

TEAM 'ADAM

The first beings created on earth were called Adam. As we read in Genesis and Moses, they are the first. At least in the beginning, God did not distinguish between the halves, man or woman. He *called their name Adam.*[2] The scriptures teach that God created male and female separately but called them Adam *collectively.* They were one, unified. God didn't instruct the man or woman separately to multiply. He talked to them both as a team, as a unit. Erastus Snow taught, "He speaks unto them as belonging together, as constituting one being, and as organized in his image and after his likeness."[3]

In Genesis, the Hebrew word *'adam* is used throughout most of the biblical allegory and means "humankind." The Hebrew noun *'ish* is more specific and carries the meaning of "one man," or even "husband." *Ha-'adam* is the plural pronoun used when speaking of "them," such as "And let *them* have dominion" or "Male and female created he them."[4]

Biblical scholars have found that *ha-'adam* was often incorrectly translated as a proper name (with a capital "A").[5] According to Strong's Lexicon, *mankind* is the most often-intended meaning in the Old Testament usage of *man* or *'adam*. So, when *'adam* is given dominion over all life in and on the earth, it is given to both Adam and Eve.

TREES OF REVELATION

The wording in both Genesis, the Hebrew text, and the book of Moses[6] indicate that Adam and Eve were united in both thought and action before partaking of the fruit, hiding after hearing God's voice, and later when both shared responsibility for their transgression. Ultimately it becomes irrelevant who yielded to temptation first because they acted as one. Many examples in the Book of Mormon reference this plurality of "man," suggesting that the Hebrew form of *'adam* (without the capital A) was used, indicating the couple worked unified and as one.[7] Even the Doctrine and Covenants states, "The devil tempted Adam, and he partook of the forbidden fruit and transgressed."[8]

Eve partook first, but both needed to stay together, and both were expected to partake of the tree of knowledge of good and evil. In fact, one rabbinical translation of Genesis 2:9 reads that both trees were sources of prophetic visions and revelations. Instead of the traditional *to look at,* in verse 9, the phrase becomes *for vision/ revelation.*[9] As both Adam and Eve ate from the trees and partook of these sources of visions and revelations, they both become prophet and prophetess.

We first see evidence of this separation when both Adam and Eve use the singular personal pronoun *I* when accounting for their actions before the Father. "*I* was naked." "*I* hid myself." "*I* did eat."[10] Both heard the voice of God and both hid, but suddenly when an accounting is called for, their unity is quickly ruptured.

Part of our mission and requirement for progression is to find a way to become, once again, united with that other half; to become "at-one" with God the Father, His son Jesus Christ, and with our spouse. We are to overcome that natural man and ignore the temptation to seek dominion over any of our relationships, to work beyond the power struggle that begins always with *I*, and settle into the working partnership of *we*. And that successful *we* will always include the Godhead.

PARENTHOOD CHANGES 'ADAM

Moses 5:10–11 reads:

> And in that day Adam blessed God and was filled, and began to prophesy concerning all the families of the earth, saying: Blessed be the name of God, for because of *my* transgression *my* eyes are opened, and in this life *I* shall have joy, and again in the flesh *I* shall see God.
>
> And Eve, his wife, heard all these things and was glad, saying: Were it not for *our* transgression *we* never should have had seed, and never should have known good and evil, and the joy of *our* redemption, and the eternal life which God giveth unto all the obedient. (emphasis added)

Both Adam and Eve individually recognize the wisdom of the Fall and the mercy and grace of God. There are two possible interpretations of their responses (*I* versus *we*). Either Adam seems to still be learning about the necessity and lesson of unity or, more likely, he now recognizes personal accountability. Eve seems to embrace the consequences of a unified decision. Whatever the personal lessons for them, we are to remember that God has all wisdom. He knows the beginning to the end.

As for the earth, from latter-day scripture we read that the curse that was placed upon the land has been lifted as recorded in Doctrine and Covenants 61:17: "And as I, the Lord, in the beginning cursed the land, even so in the last days have I blessed it, in its time, for the use of my saints that they may partake of the fatness thereof."

Whichever way we choose to look at the consequences of both Adam and Eve's choice, the ultimate result is the same for both of them. They both are now subject to mortality and all that brings with the experiences of having a mortal body, facing good and evil, learning to navigate through the opposition in all things.

ENDNOTES

1. Shira Halevi, in *The Life Story of Adam and Havah: a New Targum of Genesis 1:26–5:5* (Aronson, 1997), 202.

2. Genesis 5:2; Moses 6:9

3. Erastus Snow, "There Is a God-Communion With Him An Inherent Craving of the Human Heart—Man in His Image—Male and Female Created He Them—Spirit and Flesh—Mortal and Immortal," *Journal of Discourses*, March 3, 1878, journalofdiscourses.com/19/40, accessed November 6, 2019. See also 2 Nephi 9:6.

4. Genesis 1:26–27. See also Jolene Edmunds Rockwood, "The Redemption of Eve," in *Sisters in Spirit: Mormon Women in Historical and Cultural Perspective*, ed. Maureen Ursenbach. Beecher and Lavina Fielding Anderson (Urbana, I: University of Illinois Press, 1992), 3–29.
   In 2 Nephi 9:6 the plurality of man is addressed as well: "And the resurrection must needs come unto *man* by reason of the fall; and the fall came by reason of transgression; and because *man* became fallen they were cut off from the presence of the Lord" (emphasis added).

5. See Ernest Lussier, "'Adam in Genesis 1, 1–4, 24", *Catholic Biblical Quarterly* 18, (1956), 137–39.

6. Moses 4:7–12

7. See 1 Nephi 5:11; Mosiah 3:11, 19; 16:3–4; Alma 42:2–4; Mormon 9:12

8. Doctrine and Covenants 29:40

9. Halevi, 95.

10. Genesis 3:10, 13

Chapter 8

THE TEMPLE—A HOUSE OF THE LORD

If you will receive wisdom,
here is wisdom.

—Doctrine and Covenants 57:3

WHY A TEMPLE?

A temple is considered a place where heaven and earth meet, where man—*'adam*—strives to align his or her will with God's.[1] It represents the mountains where anciently holy men went to commune with Heavenly Father, symbolically the closest to heaven, God, and spiritual guidance.

It must be stressed here that utmost reverence, respect, and sanctity must be used when discussing the holy temple.[2] Any such discussion in this book carefully repeats only that which has previously been printed by leaders of The Church of Jesus Christ of Latter-day Saints or canonized scripture. Certain aspects of the temple ceremony are not shared. One of the reasons we do not share everything about the temple (at least outside of the building proper) is that each individual is meant to receive for him or herself the powerfully sacred and spiritual experiences the temple ordinances offer. If we speak too casually about these, we risk the ordinances or ceremonies being taken out of context, sharing with someone who is not prepared or would treat them with disrespect, or robbing another of the gift and strength of self-discovery.

Letters written by Brigham Young suggest that the temple ceremony was not dictated by Joseph Smith, but rather that Joseph "obtained the basic endowment[3] from the writings of Abraham, which he later gave to Brigham Young, who added such instructional portions as the creation account." Brigham Young later assigned the writing of a standardized endowment ceremony script to Wilford Woodruff. Over the years any alteration in the temple ceremony—via script or dramatization—has been merely for clarification.[4]

OUR SYMBOLIC JOURNEY

In the temple, instruction is given concerning our first parents and their state in the Garden of Eden. Adam and Eve, historical figures, are used symbolically in the temple ceremony. The garden, called paradise, aptly describes our eventual eternal dwelling place if we qualify. Both the garden and eternal life (dwelling with God) are timeless. Time exists only in this mortal world, as do pain and trials.

The Garden of Eden itself served as a symbolic primordial temple:[5]

1. It was an enclosed space that was separated from the rest of the world.
2. It was planted in the east and therefore considered the "holy of holies" where God dwelt.[6]
3. The tree of life relates symbolically with the menorah described in Exodus 25:31–33.
4. The sacred rivers that flow from the garden correspond and relate to the waters gushing from Ezekiel's temple description. The temple waters, as well as the fruit, trees, leaves, and food represent and symbolize healing, life, joy, fruitful.[7]
5. It is referred to as paradise—as is the future dwelling place of the righteous—divided into three courts or degrees of glory, each progressively more sacred than the last.

We repeat this journey in the temple each time as we immerse ourselves in the imagery, symbolism, and sacredness of the endowment. Our goal is to break down the worldly cocoon that we often find ourselves in, to lay aside the cares and entrapments that disrupt our pilgrimage back home.

Brigham Young explained that the purpose of the endowment is "to receive all those ordinances in the House of the Lord, which are necessary for you, after you have departed this life, to enable you to walk back to the presence of the Father, . . . and gain your eternal exaltation in spite of earth and hell."[8] Donald W. Parry and Andrew Ehat wrote, "Seen for what it is, it is the step-by-step ascent into the Eternal Presence."[9]

GENDER EQUALITY AND DIVINE FEMININE IN THE TEMPLE

The story of Adam and Eve's expulsion from the garden is a symbolic representation of our own departure from God's presence from His "holy of holies," where we used to dwell side by side. We are to relate to the accounts as if we are Adam and Eve, respective of our own gender. Each account of this narrative serves "as a message about our need for obedience, the consequences of our sins, and our desperate need for a Savior to redeem us from our fallen condition."[10] It is also a promise of a return and reconciliation with God as we keep the covenants and commandments He has required of us. That is the message. That is the gift.

There are very few places other than the temple where there is truly no respecter of persons. Both male and female are dressed in white, symbolizing that all are equal before God and that we strive to come before the Lord as a pure and righteous people. We share desires to be better sons and daughters of Heavenly Parents, entering into nearly identical covenants. The temple itself is a sacred place where men and women are able to obtain their priesthood blessings just as Abraham (and I would surmise Sarah as well) sought his.

Power, authority, and presiding are not unique elements that are reserved for the priesthood. Both genders exercise these elements, as well as officiate in the temple, in their respective roles and duties.

THE FEMININE IN TEMPLE ARCHITECTURE

Perhaps in no other place on earth are the divine feminine and equality more accurately articulated than in the temple. Both sexes make sacred covenants and—while there are some minor differences between a few of the male and female covenants—both sexes are enlightened and empowered because of them.

Male and female aspects are present even in the architecture of the temple, especially in the ancient temple. The gospel of Philip from the Nag Hammadi[11] speaks of three buildings of sacrifice. Scholars are not sure whether they are three separate buildings, or represent a larger comprehensive structure like the Jerusalem temple.[12] This excerpt from the Nag Hammadi text reads: "The one facing west was called 'the holy.' Another facing south was called 'the holy of the holy.' The third facing east was called 'the holy of the holies,' the place where only the high priest enters. Baptism is 'the holy' building. Redemption is 'the holy of the holy.' 'The holy of the holies' is the bridal chamber."[13]

Why would the bridal chamber be designated as the holy of holies? Perhaps because the highest order we can enter into is the order of eternal marriage, or the patriarchal order, signifying that it is a most holy and sacred ordinance. "Neither is the man without the woman, neither the woman without the man, in the Lord."[14]

The prophets have taught Latter-day Saints that an integral part of obtaining eternal life and becoming like our Heavenly Parents lies within marriage, more particularly one sealed in the house of the Lord.

RIGHTS OF THE PRIESTHOOD

Where does priesthood tie in with this doctrine? When men and women receive temple ordinances and are sealed together in the new and everlasting covenant (the patriarchal order), they both enter in an "order of the priesthood."[15] As clarification, while these ordinances are priesthood ordinances, they "do not bestow ecclesiastical office on men or women."[16]

M. Russell Ballard said, "When men and women go to the temple, they are both endowed with the same power, which is priesthood power. . . . Access to the power and the blessings of the priesthood is available to all of God's children."[17]

In 2016 the Church published an essay entitled "Joseph Smith's Teachings about Priesthood, Temple, and Women." It refers to Joseph Smith speaking about establishing a "kingdom of priests" as spoken of in Exodus 19:6. Joseph Smith taught that this "kingdom of priests" would comprise both men and women who made temple covenants.[18]

In the restored Church of Jesus Christ, the priesthood is more than "the right to lead a congregation or officiate over sacramental ceremonies."[19] According to David Holland, professor at Harvard Divinity School, the priesthood is a sacred endowment that "empowers its holders to speak, act, and heal in the name of God. It *alters one's relationship to the divine*" (emphasis added). Holland admitted that, with the edict of priesthood ordination to only worthy Latter-day Saint men, feelings justifiably run high for some. But he writes that many Latter-day Saints fail to see the full meaning of what St. Paul taught in Corinthians.[20]

Holland continues, "[In the temple] women are clothed in priestly vestments . . . and pronounced priestesses. The idea is that just as men become fathers through a woman's divinely endowed maternal capacity, so women become endowed with priesthood power through that same divine marriage. Through such a marriage, men and women can both be parents, and they can both be priests—and thus, through that relationship, they both progress toward godliness."[21]

CHRIST'S ATONEMENT— A PROTECTIVE COVERING

All Christian traditions are well acquainted with two trees in the garden, recognizing them as the tree of life and the tree of good and evil. Adam and Eve both became prophet and prophetess as they ate from the trees, and in temples, both Adam and Eve serve as high priests: priest and priestess. Many rabbinical interpretations agree that the garments Elohim clothed Adam and Eve in (see Genesis 3:21) were considered priestly garments, robes of honor.[22]

In fact, some intriguing varying translations of the Hebrew Genesis 3:21 read:[23]

> Then Yahweh Elohim provided leather garments
> inner garments
> garments next to the skin
> garments of light
> enlightenment
> Righteousness

Because women are endowed with priesthood power through the patriarchal order, these translations carry a greater measure of richness as well as authenticity. Both men and women are endowed with this priestly power, as well as light and enlightenment as provided by Elohim and Jesus Christ. And they both now have put on a new man—and woman—"which after God is created in righteousness and true holiness."[24]

The temple gives us an experience and opportunity to remember the Lord. Beyond reuniting Adam and Eve, the most important aspect and central figure of the temple and temple ceremony is Christ Himself. The ceremony, the lessons, tokens, signs (as spoken of by Brigham Young), clothing, and garments are to bring remembrance to our minds of our commitments, covenants, separation from and reparation with God, our fallen nature, nakedness, and our need for the covering of Christ's Atonement.

This Atonement of Jesus Christ not only offers protection but also grace, an extended power that allows us to change and progress to become like our Heavenly Parents. These garments are a reminder of who we are—children of Deity and rightful heirs in God's kingdom.

ENDNOTES

1. Raising an arm "to the square" is another such symbolism that represents the meeting of the vertical (*'adam*) and horizontal (God) axis.

2. "No jot, iota, or tittle of the temple rites is otherwise than uplifting and sanctifying. In every detail the endowment ceremony contributes to covenants of morality of life, consecration of person to high ideals, devotion to truth, patriotism to nation, and allegiance to

God. The blessings of the House of the Lord are restricted to no privileged class; every member of the Church may have admission to the temple with the right to participate in the ordinances thereof, if he [or she] come duly accredited as of worthy life and conduct" (James E. Talmage, *The House of the Lord*, 84).

3. *Endowment* is a Latin word that means "a gift of power from God. Worthy members of the Church can receive a gift of power through ordinances in the temple that gives them the instruction and covenants of the Holy Priesthood that they need in order to attain exaltation. The endowment includes instruction about the plan of salvation" (Guide to the Scriptures, ChurchofJesusChrist.org/scriptures/gs/endowment).

4. Jolene Edmunds Rockwood, "The Redemption of Eve," in *Sisters in Spirit: Mormon Women in Historical and Cultural Perspective*, ed. Maureen Ursenbach. Beecher and Lavina Fielding Anderson (Urbana, I: University of Illinois Press, 1992), 3–29, footnote 89. See also L. John Nuttal, Diary, February 7, 1877, as quoted in Hyrum Andrus, *God, Man and the Universe*, 2nd ed. 4 vols. (Salt Lake City, Utah: Bookcraft, 1970) 1:333–34, footnote. In 1877, under the direction and request of Brigham Young, a standardized endowment ceremony script was written by Wilford Woodruff and George Q. Cannon. See Boyd K. Packer, *The Holy Temple*, 191–94.

5. As described by Shira Halevi, in *The Life Story of Adam and Havah: A New Targum of Genesis 1:26–5:5* (Aronson, 1997), 112–115.

6. Jubilees 8:19

7. Ezekiel 47:1–12

8. Brigham Young, *Discourses of Brigham Young*, 416.

9. Donald W. Parry and Andrew Ehat, "Who Shall Ascend into the House of the Lord?' Sesquicentennial Reflections of a Sacred Day: 4 May 1842," in *Temples of the Ancient World: Ritual and Symbolism* (Salt Lake City, UT: Deseret Book, 1994), 58. See also Truman G. Madsen, in *The Radiant Life* (Salt Lake City, UT: Bookcraft, 1994).

10. Alonzo L. Gaskill, *The Savior & the Serpent: Unlocking the Doctrine of the Fall* (Salt Lake City, UT: Deseret Book, 2005), 26–27.

11. The Nag Hammadi texts were discovered in 1945 by Egyptian farmers near the town of Nag Hammadi in upper Egypt. They are a thirteen–volume library of mid-fourth century texts. They contain more than fifty texts, and some were composed as early as the second century (biblical archaeology.org).

12. Mihail Neamțu, Andrei Pleşu, and Bogdan Tătaru-Cazaban, *Memory, Humanity, and Meaning: Selected Essays in Honor of Andrei Pleşu's Sixtieth Anniversary* (Bucharest: Zeta Books, 2009), 75.

13. James N. Robinson, ed., "The Gospel of Philip," in *The Nag Hammadi Library* (New York, NY: Harper Collins, 1990), 151.

14. 1 Corinthians 11:11

15. Doctrine and Covenants 131:1–4

16. Joseph Smith's Teachings about Priesthood, Temple, and Women, ChurchofJesusChrist.org/topics/joseph-smiths-teachings-about-priesthood-temple-and-women?lang=eng.

17. M. Russell Ballard, "Men and Women in the Work of the Lord," *New Era*, April 2014, 4.

18. "Joseph Smith's Teachings about Priesthood, Temple, and Women," churchofjesuschrist.org/study/manual/gospel-topics-essays/joseph-smiths-teachings-about-priesthood-temple-and-women?lang=eng Latter-day Saints believed that the temple rites were the means of fulfilling the mandate to become "a kingdom of priests, and an holy nation." Joseph Smith spoke of this purpose in his March 31, 1842, address to the Relief Society, saying he would "make of this Society a kingdom of priests [as] in Enoch's day—as in Pauls day." His statement made an impression. Bathsheba W. Smith later recounted that Joseph Smith "wanted to make us, as the women were in Paul's day, 'A kingdom of priestesses.'" She then explained, "We have that ceremony in our endowments as Joseph taught" (churchhistorianspress.org/the-first-fifty-years-of-relief-society/front-matter/introduction?lang=eng#note63).

19. Paul Massari, "Exclusion or God's Plan: Interview with David F. Holland," Harvard Divinity School, June 25, 2014, hds.harvard.edu/news/2014/06/25/exclusion-or-god%E2%80%99s-plan#

20. 1 Corinthians 11:11

21. Paul Massari, "Exclusion or God's Plan: Interview with David F. Holland," Harvard Divinity School, June 25, 2014, hds.harvard.edu/news/2014/06/25/exclusion-or-god%E2%80%99s-plan#

22. See Bemidbar Rabbah IV.8 It's also interesting to note that Luke 24:49 speaks of the disciples "endued with power from on high," a Greek word that means "endow" or "to clothe," both central themes of the temple experience.

23. Halevi, 206.

24. Ephesians 4:24

Chapter 9

THE SACRED OFFICE OF MARRIAGE

Marriage is more than your love for each other. . . . In your love you see only your two selves in the world, but in marriage you are a link in the chain of the generations, which God causes to come and to pass away to his glory, and calls into his kingdom. In your love you see only the heaven of your own happiness, but in marriage you are placed at a post of responsibility towards the world and mankind. Your love is your own private possession, but marriage is more than something personal—it is a status, an office. Just as it is the crown, and not merely the will to rule, that makes the king, so it is marriage, and not merely your love for each other, that joins you together in the sight of God and man. . . . So love comes from you, but marriage from above, from God.[1]

—Dietrich Bonhoeffer, *Letters and Papers from Prison*

WHAT GOD HATH JOINED

When Eve partakes of the fruit, she and Adam are separated by their very different physical natures. Her body is now mortal (as opposed to his still immortal

61

one), subject not only to death and corruption (in the scriptural sense of the body exposed to decay), but also, now God would separate her and Adam, as she would be forced to leave both the garden and Adam.

Satan won the battle, but Eve's quick thinking and clever arguments will ensure that the war is far from lost. She reminds Adam of the commandment that the two were to "be fruitful, and multiply, and replenish the earth,"[2] a commandment that he could not keep with her banished from the garden.

M. Russell Ballard said, "It takes a man and a woman to create a family, and it takes men and women to carry out the work of the Lord. A husband and wife righteously working together complete each other."[3] Doctrine and Covenants 88:119 speaks of "establishing a house" and is often quoted in Latter-day Saint culture as a template for not only the building of a temple, but also of a home and family. Each marriage partner has equal but specific gender-based roles and responsibilities in establishing that house. And, as the Family Proclamation has stated, each has an obligation to assist the other in those roles, to be one another's highest and best advocate. Husbands and wives have the opportunity, and challenge, to become a divine pair. They use their parallel attributes to become one.

Sharon Eubank, first counselor in the General Relief Society Presidency, shared, "I do not think 'sealing' is an idly chosen word. And it is asking us to become unified in the same way that we are unified in this way. And so it takes probably a lifetime and beyond to create this unified, divine pair. But it is a transition from self-interest, and worried about me, to worrying about the unit. And basically we are saying in our sealed, divine unit – 'I trust you and I have your best interests at heart. . . . I will look out for you and I will look for your greatest good.'"[4]

Adam and Eve were created for each other, companions to walk side by side in the lone and dreary world, protecting each other and their children in their respective roles and in their divinely appointed way. They are help meets for each other, protecting and providing what the other needs but cannot attain for themselves.

THE DIVINE PAIR

Despite the past inequalities that existed in marriages in many cultures around the world, we can move forward to uniting, binding, and restoring what was lost in Eden. Mortality seems to present the perfect conditions for a husband and wife to work on becoming coequal partners. The ultimate outcome is to create a beautiful interdependence with each other, maintaining a check and balances, if you will, of counseling as full partners with the family and in the home. They are to trust each other to keep their covenants and respective promises to the LORD.

The scriptural image of "cleaving" is similar to the idea of bone cleaving or adhering to flesh. This Hebrew verb is often used when expressing the idea of two separate entities attaching closely to each other yet preserving their uniqueness, of becoming interdependent, such as of a human yearning to be one with his or her God.

Some cultures have taken the Adam and Eve story and created a template that was not designed by God. The mandate for the man to leave his parents and cleave unto his wife stands in bold contrast against the erroneous definition some have perpetuated of a *patriarchal society*. From Genesis 2:24 we glean three important concepts:

1. Woman (Eve) was created as an equal but independent creation alongside Adam.
2. Woman (Eve) is not a possession of man (Adam) even in marriage.
3. Achieving this unity and oneness, modeling the oneness of Christ and Elohim, is the goal and commandment for both of them.[5]

As we look into the separate covenants that each makes with their Creator, we can see that though the covenants are different, they are the same in purpose: to bring unity to that which was separated and heal that which was broken. They are covenants that strive for the equal partnership of Adam and Eve and to bring both of them as One, and individual entities, back into the presence of *the Lord* (Christ and Elohim)—their one true template of a unified partnership.

The Gospel of Philip (from the Nag Hammadi Library) speaks of this healing: "If the woman had not separated from the man she should not die with the man. His separation became the beginning of death. Because of this Christ came to repair the separation which was from the beginning and again unite the two, and to give life to those who died as a result of the separation and unite them. But the woman is united to her husband in the bridal chamber. Indeed *those who have united in the bridal chamber will no longer be separated.*"[6]

The bridal chamber symbolizes "the holy of holies." Marriage was meant to be for eternity and the highest order any man or woman could enter into. Philip also speaks of being "clothed in perfect light"[7] and "not able to detain them."[8]

"One will clothe himself in this light sacramentally in the union,"[9] of which he refers to the union of man and woman; that of eternal marriage.

We are in a great training ground, placed here by the Great Creator, to learn how to govern and counsel and work together as one unit, modeling ourselves after God's government ("The Father and I are one").[10]

ORDINANCES AND OUR FIRST LIVING ENDOWMENT

When speaking about keeping the ordinance of marriage, one should look at what an ordinance is: "a sacred, formal act performed by the authority of the priesthood."[11] Some ordinances are considered saving ordinances, as they are essential to exaltation. The marriage sealing is one of these higher ordinances and is performed in the temple. This sealing is also known as a temple marriage. When one is sealed to a spouse in the temple, they make solemn covenants with the Lord and with each other. Priesthood authority performs this and other ordinances.

Boyd K. Packer, in a speech about ordinances at BYU (1980), discussed the definitions of three words: order, ordain, and ordinance.

There comes the impression that an ordinance, to be valid, must be done in proper order.

Order—To put in ranks or rows, in proper sequence or relationship.

Ordain—The process of putting things in rows or proper relationship.

Ordinance—The ceremony by which things are put in proper order."[12]

One of the names that eternal marriage is given is patriarchal *order*. But what if we looked at birth as an ordinance, as our first living endowment? It fits in the proper order of things, as we need physical bodies to receive a fulness of joy,[13] and it is required to become like our Heavenly Parents.[14] When members of the Church enter into the new and everlasting covenant of marriage—the patriarchal order—women become priestesses alongside their male counterparts, the priests. Part of this ordinance of marriage—the mission—is to bring spirit children to earth, clothing them in a physical body and giving them a temple[15] to dwell in, entering into (by birth) the covenant. This is the proper order that ordinances and covenants set out for us.

President Spencer W. Kimball said, "We do not raise children just to please our vanity. We bring children into the world to become kings and queens, and priests and priestesses for our Lord."[16]

Melvin J. Ballard promised, "All the honor and glory that can come to men or women . . . is but a dim thing whose luster shall fade in comparison to the high honor. . . . The ever-enduring happiness that shall come to the woman who fulfills the first great duty and mission that devolves upon her to become the mother of the sons and daughters of God."[17]

IDEOLOGY VERSUS ORDER

Why is marriage and having a family so important, especially in our day of sexual revolution where the ideology is taught that paperwork is not needed for two people to love each other nor to begin a family? First and foremost is the truth taught by Boyd K. Packer—order. God is a god of order. Relationships are to be put in the proper order, the order that has been established by Heavenly Parents.

Besides, Elder D. Todd Christofferson taught that marriage "has never been just about the love and happiness of adults."[18] Marriage and family are the best foundational unit for the fulfillment of personal joy as well as society's best chance as it centers in God's template created in the very beginning. It is Heavenly Father who created our first parents in His image and joined them together (as husband and wife) to "multiply and replenish the earth." Anything else is merely a social experiment at odds with God's plan that will fail time and again. Marriage is "as much a part of the plan of happiness as the Fall and the Atonement."[19]

As Elder D. Todd Christofferson also said, "Each individual carries the divine image, but it is in the matrimonial union of male and female as one that we attain perhaps the most complete meaning of our having been made in the image of God—male and female. Neither we nor any other mortal can alter this divine order of matrimony. It is not a human invention."[20]

Despite what the world teaches, true happiness is most likely found within the gospel, following the teachings of Jesus Christ. If two people are sincerely interested in a happy marriage and family, they will build their foundation on these principles taught within the gospel, not the least of which are forgiveness and respect.

Most of the images and templates in the gospel are related in terms of the family: we are children of Heavenly Parents, we strive for eternal marriage and eternal families, entrance into the celestial kingdom is contingent upon marriage in the house of the Lord, and we are promised that we too can become like our Heavenly Parents with the creation of spirit children of our own in the eternities.[21]

ENDNOTES

1. Dietrich Bonhoeffer, *Letters and Papers from Prison,* ed. Eberhard Bethge (1953), 42–43.
2. Genesis 1:28
3. M. Russell Ballard, "Men and Women and Priesthood Power." *Ensign*, September 2014.

4. Sharon Eubank, "'This Is a Woman's Church.'" FairMormon, August 8, 2014, www.fairmormon.org/perspectives/fair-conferences/2014–fairmormon-conference/womans-church.

5. Dawn Hall Anderson, Marie Cornwall, and Jolene Edmunds Rockwood, "Eve's Role in the Creation and the Fall to Mortality," in *Women and the Power within: to See Life Steadily and See It Whole* (Salt Lake City, UT: Deseret Book, 1991), 49–62.

6. James N. Robinson, ed., "The Gospel of Philip," in *The Nag Hammadi Library* (New York, NY: Harper Collins, 1990), 151, emphasis added.

7. Ibid.

8. Ibid.

9. Ibid.

10. Doctrine and Covenants 93:3

11. ChurchofJesusChrist.org/topics/ordinances?lang=eng

12. Boyd K. Packer, "Ordinances—Boyd K. Packer," BYU Speeches, speeches.byu.edu/talks/boyd-k-packer_ordinances/, accessed November 11, 2019.

13. Doctrine and Covenants 93:33–34

14. Doctrine and Covenants 130:22

15. 1 Corinthians 6:19

16. Spencer W. Kimball, "Train Up a Child," The Church of Jesus Christ of Latter-day Saints, ChurchofJesusChrist.org/ensign/1978/04/train-up-a-child?lang=eng, accessed November 30, 2019.

17. Bryant S. Hinckley and Melvin Joseph Ballard, *Sermons and Missionary Services of Melvin Joseph Ballard* (Salt Lake City: Deseret Book, 1949).

18. D. Todd Christofferson, "Why Marriage, Why Family," The Church of Jesus Christ of Latter-day Saints, April 2015, ChurchofJesusChrist.org/general-conference/2015/04/why-marriage-why-family?lang=eng.

19. Ibid. Elder Christofferson also offered the following commentary: "People may be loyal to one another in nonmarital relationships, and children can be born and raised, sometimes quite successfully, in other than a married two-parent family environment. But on average and in the majority of cases, evidence of the social benefits of marriage and of the comparatively superior

outcomes for children in families headed by a married man and woman is extensive. . . . [Quoting Nicholas Eberstadt] Yes, children are resilient and all that. But the flight from family most assuredly comes at the expense of the vulnerable young. That same flight also has unforgiving implications for the vulnerable old." (See "The Global Flight from the Family," *Wall Street Journal,* Feb. 21, 2015, wsj.com/articles/nicholas-eberstadt-the-global-flight-from-the-family-1424476179.)

20. Ibid.
21. Dallin H. Oaks, "Priesthood Authority in the Family and the Church," The Church of Jesus Christ of Latter-day Saints, 2005, ChurchofJesusChrist.org/general-conference/2005/10/priesthood-authority-in-the-family-and-the-church?lang=eng.

Chapter 10
WHAT IS A WIFE?

*As His final creation, the crowning of His
glorious work, He created woman. I like to
regard Eve as His masterpiece after all that had
gone before, the final work before He rested from
His labors. I do not regard her as being
in second place to Adam.*[1]

—Gordon B. Hinckley

'EZER KENEGDO—HELP MEET
OR HELPMEET?

The Hebrew in Genesis 2:18 translates as "It is not good that
the man should be alone; I will make him an help ['*ezer*]
meet [*kenegdo*] for him."

"Help meet" has been a misunderstood and distorted term
in the Bible. In our English culture, the overtone for the word
help or *helper* is often one of a lower or lesser status. But the
Hebrew form suggests not just an equal but possibly one of a
superior status. The context of '*ezer* in other Bible passages refers
to God or of a military ally giving help or aid.[2] Jean Higgins,
former Assistant Professor of Religion at Smith College, noted,

"Of forty-five occurrences of the word [*'ezer*] in the [Septuagint], forty-two unmistakably refer to help from a stronger one."[3]

The biblical scholar David Freedman writes that the Hebrew word *'ezer* is actually a merge of two different roots. One root means "to rescue or save"; the other means "to be strong." It used to carry the rich nuance of both meanings—to be rescued or saved by one who is strong. Now, however, it has been dumbed down to simply "to help," all but obliterating the vivid and rich overtone that once existed.[4]

And what of *kenegdo*? *Kenegdo* was only used one time in the Old Testament (see Genesis 2:18). Jolene Edmunds Rockwood explained that it is important to follow its usage in the Mishnaic Hebrew:[5] "*Kenegdo*, then, means *equal to*, and the entire phrase *'ezer kenegdo* means *power or strength equal to*. Thus, when God makes *ha-'dam* into two beings, he creates woman, a power or strength equal to man."[6] Adding the *kenegdo* modifies *'ezer* into one of equal status.

Despite how cultures interpret the role of a wife, Eve was definitely created and meant to hold her own identity, to be interdependent with Adam. To be one with another human being is a great honor, as well as a challenge. But the rewards and blessings far outweigh any price that is to be paid or effort that is expended on behalf of the marriage relationship.

A WIFE IS A WIFE IS A WIFE . . . OR IS SHE?

God's creation of Eve or of woman was never meant to merely be a man's helper (which in our culture conjures images of "Hand me the wrench, Dear.") Rather, Eve was created as a powerful and strong *partner* to man, a unified *'adam*. Moses 5:1 reads, "And Eve . . . did labor *with* him." *With* is a significant word in this passage. It signifies more than just physical labor but also cooperation, support, and a common purpose and goal.

Samuel L. Terrien said, "The creation of the woman [is] a gift for the completion and perfection of the human realm of being. Man receives woman as his true mate, his companion, even the provider of his existential succor. . . . Far from being a subordinated or menial servant, woman is the savior of man."[7]

Once again we run into cultural overlays with the King James translation and their seventeenth-century English usage of the word *meet*. Over the years, readers began hyphenating the two words into "help-meet," thus totally changing the meaning and context, eventually morphing this into "help-mate," then helpmate, then simply "wife." This term never existed in the King James Version, nor in the original Hebrew. According to the *American Heritage Dictionary*, "In the 17th Century the two words 'help' and 'meet' in this passage were mistaken for one word, applying to Eve, and thus 'helpmeet' came to mean 'a wife.' Then in the 18th century, in a misguided attempt to make sense of the word, the spelling 'helpmate' was introduced."[8]

CLOSING THE GAP

Language, we see, is incredibly powerful, and with the addition of one tiny, seemingly insignificant symbol, an entire gender can be marginalized. But what is more disturbing is that the reverse was accomplished. The translators twisted the original biblical meaning, inserting a definition to fit and confirm to an already existing cultural bias, to justify a gender marginalization that was already well underway. For example, what if we took the "righteous deeds" Paul was teaching the Gentiles about in Acts 26:20 ("and do works meets for repentance") and called them "worksmeets"?[9]

There is a wide definitional gap between a "helpmate" and "savior." Additionally, as we look at the Greek word for "helper or helpmate"—as it is used in Genesis 2:18—it is *boēthos* and implies superior strength, a "helper in dangers and in adversities, as one who repels adverse forces."[10] In fact, of the forty-five occurrences of *boēthos* in the Greek Old Testament, forty-two are translated to refer to "a stronger one, in no way needing help."[11]

Lest the reader confuse the author's intent, neither sex is above the other. Eve was created specifically to complete Adam; to complete and complement and *save* him in a way no other creation properly could. Eve was created to be a co-savior *with* Adam.

THE RIB AND ISH—
"MAN OF HIGHER DEGREE"

The Hebrew word for rib—*tsela*—occurs thirty-two times in the Bible. Of those thirty-two incidents, only in Genesis 2:21–11 is *tsela* translated as "rib," a body part. In all other translations *tsela* is part of the construction of a tabernacle, temple, or ark of the covenant—all, interestingly enough, structural elements of a temple.[12]

Genesis 2:23 reads, "She shall be called Woman, because she was taken out of Man." Shira Halevi said, "The Hebrew word for man in this verse is *ish*, not *adam*. . . . This is the first time *ish* occurs in the Torah. Up to this point in Scripture, *man*, *Adam*, and *mankind* are consistently represented by the word *adam*."[13]

In many of the scriptural cases, both *ish* and *adam* are used interchangeably, as they are both generic, meaning *man*. But there are different levels of meanings to both of these terms. For instance, *adam* is associated with earth or dirt, meaning he is earthy or red, made of blood. With these associations he is at a lower level than Man of Holiness. In Strong's Hebrew Lexicon, the word *adam* refers to a common sort, man of lower degree.[14] This is the most common use in the scriptures. But when the Hebrew word *ish* is used, it is for the man of high degree. According to Halevi, in scripture, "such men as prophets, patriarchs, priests, temple workmen, royal officials, and men of wisdom are always called *ish*—never adam."[15] Halevi also said that "an ish is an elevated man, often holy. A literal translation for this level of meaning would be 'higher man', 'holy man', or 'man of holiness.'"[16] *Ish*, interestingly enough, is also associated with *esh,* referring to "holy fire."[17]

HOLINESS, FIRE, AND THE PUNCHLINE

So, how does this relate to Eve? If he were really going to give her a name that reflected that she was literally created from his flesh, that is, calling her after himself, Adam, as Halevi states, "would have named her *Adamah*, the feminine counterpart to his own name."

Instead, he calls her by a title of great honor, "*Ishah*, the feminine counterpart to *ish*, with all its allusions to *holiness and fire*."[18]

Ish can have several layers of meanings—prophet, a wise man, a divine being, or even God. But "there is another meaning for *ish*, a meaning never labeled *adam* in Scripture," Halevi asserts, and that is "*a man who marries a woman.*"[19] Interestingly enough, a woman's *ish* is translated as "husband."[20]

Halevi continues: "When an *adam* marries an *ishah*, a woman, his status is immediately elevated to that of an *ish*—*a man of higher degree. He becomes more like the Divine Being in whose image he was created.*"[21] So when Elohim instructs *adam* to "Awake! Arise" (as per Halevi's translation cited in chapter 6), He is introducing *adam/Adam* to "His [God's] final creation, the crowning of His glorious work . . . His masterpiece after all that had gone before, the final work before He rested from His labors."[22]

Adam is to "arise" because he is standing before one who is of a high status, and in his union with her will be raised to one of higher status as well. With Eve, the mother of all living, he is able to do that which he could not do without her, that which is the "most godlike activity available to human beings—create life."[23]

Women bring men life.

In all the roles that a faithful woman is engaged in, the role of *wife* takes priority over everything else, including that of mother.[24] Many are tempted to set aside and neglect the marriage and husband for a time, in favor of catering to the children. As noble as motherhood is, marriage is not to be sacrificed for it. Much can be taught the children through the example of the loving companionship of a righteous father and mother.

As Joseph Fielding Smith taught, "The Lord said he would give the man a companion who would be a help meet for him: that is, a help who would answer all the requirements, not only of companionship, but also through whom the fullness of the purposes of the Lord could be accomplished regarding the mission of man through mortal life and into eternity."[25]

ENDNOTES

1. Gordon B. Hinckley, "Daughters of God," The Church of Jesus Christ of Latter-day Saints, Churchofjesuschrist.org/study/general-conference/1991/10/daughters-of-god?lang=eng, accessed November 30, 2019.

2. We have such references in Psalm 30:10 or 54:4, where David refers to God as his Helper, the context hardly referring to God as an inferior being.

3. Jean Higgins, "Anastasius Sinaita and the Superiority of the Woman," *Journal of Biblical Literature* 97, no. 2 (1978): 255.
Jolene Rockwood states that "the other usages of 'ezer in the Old Testament show that in most cases, God is an 'ezer to human beings," which questions whether "helper" is accurate in any of the translations ("The Redemption of Eve"). For instance, see Deuteronomy 33:29, 33:26; Psalm 70:5, 121:2 (All KJV).

4. 'Ezer is used as "savior" eight of the twenty-one times in the Hebrew Bible. Later on, the two meanings were merged into our present-day usage of "to help." As we look at the way the word *'ezer* was used in other Old Testament passages, a more accurate translation would be "strength," "power," or even "savior" (R. David Freedman, "Woman, A Power Equal to Man," BAR 09:01 (Jan/Feb 1983)/ Biblical Archaeology Society, 2002). See Deuteronomy 33:26, 29.
See also Beverly Campbell, in *Eve and the Choice Made in Eden* (Salt Lake City, UT: Desert Book Company, 2009), 24; Diana Webb, "Eve as a 'help meet'—What Does That Mean?" *Meridian Magazine*, September 28, 2011.

5. "Mishnaic Hebrew is one of the few Hebrew dialects found in the Talmud . . . Mishnaic Hebrew I, which was a spoken language, and . . . Mishnaic Hebrew II, which was a literary language only" (en.wikipedia.org/wiki/Mishnaic_Hebrew).

6. Dawn Hall Anderson, Marie Cornwall, and Jolene Edmunds Rockwood, "Eve's Role in the Creation and the Fall to Mortality," in *Women and the Power within: to See Life Steadily and See It Whole* (Salt Lake City, UT: Deseret Book, 1991), 49–62. See also Freedman.

7. Samuel L. Terrien, in *Till the Heart Sings: a Biblical Theology of Manhood and Womanhood* (Grand Rapids, MI: W.B. Eerdmans

Pub. Co., 2004), 10. Also take note of the lower case "s" in savior, indicating that the author is not suggesting woman is equal with or surpasses Christ.

8. *American Heritage Dictionary*, second college edition (Boston: Houghton Mifflin, 1982), 604. See also oxforddictionaries.com/us/definition/american_english/helpmate.

9. Daniel Peterson, "How Was Eve an Help Meet for Adam?" *Deseret News*, August 22, 2013.

10. Higgins, 255.

11. In Jean Higgins, "Anastasius Sinaita and the Superiority of the Woman," footnote 19 states: "God is the *boēthos* in Exod 15:2; 18:4; Deut 33:7, 26, 29; Judg 5:23: 1 Kgdms 7:12; Esth 4:17(1); Job 22:25; and in twenty-four occurrences in Psalms. Also in Sir 51:2; (36:29?); Isa 8:13; 17:1; 25:4; 50:7; 2 Macc 3:39. *Boēthos* stands in parallel with the name of God in 2 Kgdms 22:42. It denotes a helper of the weak in Job 29:12 and a helper in battle in Isa 63:5: "I looked, but there was no helper (*boēthos*); I was appalled, but there was no one to uphold; so my own arm brought me victory and my wrath upheld me."

12. Shira Halevi, in *The Life Story of Adam and Havah: a New Targum of Genesis 1:26–5:5* (Aronson, 1997), 136.

13. Halevi, 145.

14. blueletterbible.org/lang/lexicon/lexicon.cfm?t=k-jv&strongs=h120
Lexicon:: Strong's H120—adam. We also see this in other scriptural passages such as when adam is used in parallel phrases with earthly matter and animals. See for instance Genesis 6:7, 7:21, 23; Exodus 9:25, 12:12, 13:15; Leviticus 24:21, 27:28; Numbers 3:13.

15. Halevi, 147. *Ish* has also been used when referring to angels or divine messengers.

16. Halevi, 147. See also Moses 6:57.

17. Strong's Hebrew: 784 and 799 (in which the short definition of 799 means *lightning*).

18. Haveli, 148, emphasis added.

19. Ibid., 149, emphasis added.

20. Genesis 29, 32, 34, 30:15, 20; Numbers 30:7; Deuteronomy 21:23, 24:3.

21. Halevi, 149.
22. Hinckley, ibid.
23. Halevi, 150.
24. Harold B. Lee and Clyde J. Williams, *The Teachings of Harold B. Lee* (Salt Lake City, UT: The Church of Jesus Christ of Latter-day Saints, 2015).
25. Joseph Fielding Smith, *Doctrines of Salvation*, vol. 2 (Salt Lake City, UT: Bookcraft, 1998).

.

Chapter 11
MOTHER OF ALL LIVING

*When Eve was brought unto Adam, he became
filled with the Holy Spirit, and gave her the most
sanctified, the most glorious of appellations. He
called her Eva—that is to say, the Mother of All.
He did not style her wife, but simply mother—
mother of all living creatures. In this consists the
glory and the most precious ornament of woman.*

—Martin Luther

Adam addresses this newly created female Eve, meaning "the mother of all living" before she ever gave birth. Notice that it means mother of *all* living, not just mankind, not just peopling the earth. She gives life to *all* living things. Because of her choice, and then consequently giving the fruit to Adam, she initiated the change that affected the entire earth and all living things on and in it. Everything associated with the earth fell from the presence of God along with the first humans. All living things are now able to create life, whereas before they merely existed in suspended animation. Professor Valerie M. Hudson said, "It is through women that souls journey to mortality and gain their agency, and in general it is through the nurturing of women . . . that the light of Christ is awakened within each soul."[1]

STEWARDSHIP OF THE FIRST TREE

There exist different narratives of the Creation as well as the Fall of Adam and Eve, each with their own perspective and details.[2] Valerie Hudson suggests that Eve may actually have been foreordained to be the first to partake of the fruit of the tree of knowledge. Elohim could have easily called this the tree of mortality, as partaking meant "to enter into mortality with a mortal body, to enter in to full agency, and to have awakened in us the light of Christ."

Dr. Hudson continues: "The fruit of the First Tree symbolizes the gift that women give to every soul that chooses the plan of Christ. It symbolizes the role and power of women in the Great Plan of Happiness. It was not, in this view, right or proper for Adam to partake first from the fruit of the First Tree. It was not his role to give the gift of the fruit of the First Tree to others. It is interesting to think that even Adam, who was created before Eve, entered into full mortality and full agency by accepting the gift of the First Tree from the hand of a woman. In a sense, *Adam himself was born of Eve.*"[3]

We can just as accurately name that first tree the tree of lives, as that was one of the consequences that it provided to Adam and Eve when they partook. They were now mortal and possessed the power and ability to create new lives.

Eve brought life to Adam, both before and after giving him the fruit. When Adam was first introduced to Eve, he was glad, joyful. His presence in the garden now had meaning. In addition to giving him posterity and providing mortal bodies for us, Eve provided light and life into the garden, into the fallen world, and into Adam's world. She was, in part, created for Adam. She was created to help him achieve, to become what he was meant to become.

Douglas Clark argues that Eve "knew that Adam had been placed in a situation in which he could not, without Eve's help, achieve his potential, for the command not to eat the fruit had come only to him. It was up to her to take the step that Adam could not take. Only if she ate *first* would he have to eat in order to obey the first great command to multiply. She must eat so her husband could become what he had been created to be, the father of the human race. Eve must eat for his sake and for hers, for the sake of their marriage and mankind."[4]

THE RIGHTS OF THE WOMAN
AND THE PARTNERSHIP

Adam did not have the right to withhold Eve's ability to conceive a child any more than he had the right to demand that she did. Her natural desires were to have children, and the ultimate (albeit not sole) choice should rest upon the woman (Eve) as she and her daughters will bear the consequences (physical and emotional pain) of pregnancy and birth. If the reading of Genesis is used, then in all likelihood, Adam was with Eve when she partook of the fruit. He stood to the side and allowed her to make that choice. If other narratives of the allegory are used, the reader will believe that Eve was alone with Satan and she made the choice without consulting Adam. Part of the mission and challenge of marriage is to move forward *together*, consulting and counseling *together,* especially in decisions that affect both partners.

Jewish tradition is in harmony with Church doctrine, in that Eve was not physically capable of conceiving until after the Fall. Shira Halevi writes, "Remember, the Garden is also timeless. Without the progression of time, neither death nor birth can occur. Old age and fetal development, as well as the growth and maturity of a baby to adulthood, are all dependent on the forward movement of time—of days and months and years. . . . Therefore birth and death, those extreme opposites of mortality, could not exist."[5]

STEWARDSHIP OF THE SECOND TREE

Men and women are equal in the eyes of God, but they are given different roles and stewardships. We have thus far discussed the first of two trees—namely, the tree of knowledge of good and evil—and the hypothesis that Eve had stewardship over this.

Adam—and *man*kind—are given stewardship over the priesthood, the covenants and ordinances that are necessary to enter back into God's presence. This is symbolized in the second tree, the tree of life. The fruit of this tree represents immortality and eternal life—living forever in the presence of Elohim and Jesus Christ (and, by an unspoken understanding, this includes the presence of Heavenly Mother). Priesthood ordinances are a necessary step in our progression, partaking of the crowning ordinances in the temple where a man and a woman are joined as they enter into the highest order of the Melchizedek Priesthood, that of the patriarchal order. In order to receive eternal life, life with God the Father and Mother, as well as receive eternal *lives* (posterity), we must be sealed with this priesthood power. Life and lives, both mortal and eternal, require both sexes, both stewardships,[6] both trees.

Valerie Hudson said, "Just as the veil into this life is guarded by the women, the daughters of God, so the veil that brings us home, is administered and guarded by the sons of God."[7]

Diana Webb encourages us to see the wisdom at looking "at the *whole* picture that includes both women *and* men. There are two trees and two stewardships. Both are necessary for God's plan to work."[8]

A SACRED ROLE

As we come to understand the sacred role and divine power of women, we see that the divine feminine is a sacred and godly power that is inherent in a righteous woman and not contingent upon priesthood ordination. It is a power that is equal to that of the priesthood and equal in authority.

Women must be careful and cautious regarding the temptations of the world. People in the world mock motherhood and the divinely established stewardship of a wife. Femininity is seen as weak, and motherhood is viewed as a station for one who has little ambition.[9]

We often take for granted what women do for us in our lives—our biological mothers, our adopted mothers, our sisters, and best friends. For some reason, humans often downplay the incredibly sacred and life-giving power that women have that *includes* creating mortal bodies. Some have limited vision of how we all got here, not only physically but also spiritually. The women in our lives have usually and generally awakened that light of Christ that begins this entire journey: toward the covenants, the ordinances, and to the tree of life that promises our entrance back to where we began so long ago. When Eve saw that the fruit was good,[10] we see a sacred echo of God's acknowledgment during the creation periods when He "saw that it was good."[11]

Spencer W. Kimball taught, "Mothers have a sacred role. They are partners with God, as well as with their own husbands, first in giving birth to the Lord's spirit children and then in rearing those children so they will serve the Lord and keep his commandments. Could there be a more sacred trust than to be a trustee for honorable, well-born, well-developed children?"[12]

A woman has a sacred stewardship in many roles in her lifetime: a mother, teacher, spouse, leader—all with the ability to create life in its many, varied forms.

THE DAUGHTERS OF EVE AND A DIVINE CALLING

Persecution against the Christian way of life is going to increase in these last days. The world needs more women willing to step up to their calling as a life-giver, to follow the example of Mother Eve, braving the unknown, becoming solid in the foundation of the doctrine of Christ with an obedient heart. Spencer W. Kimball said that the world needs righteous women who will "teach and help raise a sin-resistant generation,"[13] able to detect deception, and recognize evil for what it is.

President Kimball also taught:

> To be a righteous woman is a glorious thing in any age. To be a righteous woman during the winding up scenes on this earth, before the second coming of our Savior, is an especially noble calling. The righteous woman's strength and influence today can be tenfold what

it might be in more tranquil times. She has been placed here to help to enrich, to protect, and to guard the home—which is society's basic and most noble institution. Other institutions in society may falter and even fail, but the righteous woman can help to save the home, which may be the last and only sanctuary some mortals know in the midst of storm and strife.[14]

It is not always easy to express one's beliefs in a world focused on shaming. But bringing life and light is not for the faint of heart, and certainly not reserved for only the hearth, home, and altar of worship. The daughters of Eve are expected to keep their covenants, thus accessing the power promised to them by God. Like mother Eve, covenant-keeping women have access to the vision and the courage to guide their families and others to the "good fruit," mainly the blessings of the priesthood.

Pat Holland, wife of Elder Jeffrey R. Holland, said, "If your role or assignment is a supportive one—and many of us [both male and female] will often have that role—we must study and prepare ourselves enough to articulate to the world that we are not apologizing for strengthening the home, but are rather pursuing our highest priorities, personally, socially, and theologically."[15]

Spencer W. Kimball best articulated it this way:

> My dear sisters, may I suggest to you something that has not been said before or at least in quite this way. Much of the major growth that is coming to the Church in the last days will come because many of the good women of the world (in whom there is often such an inner sense of spirituality) will be drawn to the Church in large numbers. This will happen to the degree that the women of the Church reflect righteousness and articulateness in their lives and to the degree that the women of the Church are seen as distinct and different—in happy ways—from the women of the world. . . . Thus it will be that female exemplars of the Church will be a significant force in both the numerical and the spiritual growth of the Church in the last days.[16]

Women are the crowning achievement, the masterpiece of God's creations.[17] This distinction is not a result of a woman's marriage, or having given birth; but simply because she *is*.

ENDNOTES

1. Valerie M. Hudson, "The Two Trees," FairMormon, 2010, fair-mormon.org/conference/august-2010/the-two-trees.

2. For instance, examining the Hebrew text of the Genesis account, the reader learns that the commandment to not partake of the tree of knowledge of good and evil is first transmitted to Adam, with Eve's knowledge of the commandment occurring at a later date. In both the Genesis and Moses accounts, the commandment to not partake of the fruit was given only to Adam, and not to Eve. Not only is she not present but she has not even been created yet. (We know from Eve's reaction to the serpent, that by that time, she was aware of the directive, and it can be assumed that Adam took it upon himself to relay this commandment to Eve. From what we have in the written scriptural narrative, there is no evidence that the commandment to abstain was meant for both. Adam assumed it was for everyone, including his new companion.

   Jewish/Biblical scholar Shira Halevi suggests that, since Adam passed the commandment on to Eve without authorization, Eve's partaking of the fruit was no sin, because God had not directly commanded her not to eat it.

3. Hudson, ibid., emphasis added.

4. E. Douglas Clark, *Echoes of Eden: Eternal Lessons from Our First Parents* (American Fork, UT: Covenant Communications, 2010).

5. Shira Halevi, in *The Life Story of Adam and Havah: a New Targum of Genesis 1:26–5:5* (Aronson, 1997), 174–75.

   Halevi also suggests that just as God and Adam noted that the Garden of Eden would be lonely for Adam without Eve, Eve realizes that Eden is not really paradise without children.

6. Elder M. Russell Ballard of the Quorum of the Twelve Apostles taught: "Men and women, though spiritually equal, are entrusted with different but equally significant roles. . . . Men are given stewardship over the sacred ordinances of the priesthood. To women, God gives stewardship over bestowing and nurturing mortal life, including providing physical bodies for God's spirit children and guiding those children toward a knowledge of gospel truths. These stewardships, equally sacred and important, do not involve any false ideas about domination or subordination" (ChurchofJesusChrist.org/ensign/2013/04/equal-partnership-in-marriage?lang=eng).

7. Hudson, ibid.

8. Diana Webb, "Understanding Eve: The Mother of All Living," *LDS Magazine*, 2016, latterdaysaintmag.com/understanding-eve-the-mother-of-all-living/.

9. See for instance Richard G. Scott, "The Joy of Living the Great Plan of Happiness," *Ensign*, November 1996, 74–75.

10. Genesis 3:6

11. Genesis 1

12. Spencer W. Kimball and Edward L. Kimball. Essay in *The Teachings of Spencer W. Kimball* (Salt Lake City, UT: Deseret Book, 1982), 326.

13. Bonnie Oscarson quoting Russell M. Nelson, "Rise Up in Strength, Sisters in Zion," October 2016 General Conference.

14. Spencer W. Kimball, "Privileges and Responsibilities of Sisters," *Ensign*, November 1978, 103.

15. Pat Holland, "A Woman's Perspective on the Priesthood," *Ensign*, July 1980, Churchofjesuschrist.org/study/ensign/1980/07/a-womans-perspective-on-the-priesthood?lang=eng.

16. Spencer W. Kimball, "The Role of Righteous Women," The Church of Jesus Christ of Latter-day Saints, ChurchofJesus-Christ.org/general-conference/1979/10/the-role-of-righteous-women?lang=eng, accessed November 12, 2019.

17. Gordon B. Hinckley, "Daughters of God," The Church of Jesus Christ of Latter-day Saints, Churchofjesuschrist.org/study/ensign/1991/11/daughters-of-god?lang=eng, accessed November 30, 2019.

Chapter 12

THE ROLE OF A HUSBAND AND FATHER

Brethren, those who save their marriages understand that this pursuit takes time, patience, and, above all, the blessings of the Atonement of Jesus Christ. It requires you to be kind, envy not, seek not your own, not be easily provoked, think no evil, and rejoice in the truth. In other words, it requires charity, the pure love of Christ.[1]

—Dieter F. Uchtdorf

The Family Proclamation outlines—with overlapping duties—the differing roles of mothers and fathers: "By divine design, fathers are to preside over their families in love and righteousness and are responsible to provide the necessities of life and protection for their families. Mothers are primarily responsible for the nurture of their children. In these sacred responsibilities, fathers and mothers are *obligated to help one another as equal partners*"[2] (emphasis added). Doctrine and Covenants 83:2 gives women the right to "have claim on their husbands for their maintenance." Spencer W. Kimball wrote that this also includes the husband's "obligation to maintain loving affection and to provide consideration and thoughtfulness as well as food."[3] (What it means for a man to preside in the home will be discussed in greater lengths in a later chapter.)

While there are divinely designed differences between men and women, God did not ordain them to be divided but united in their delegated roles. Jewish legends reveal a great deal about this time period in the garden before Adam and Eve partook of the fruit.

Hugh Nibley said, "The tradition is that the two were often apart in the Garden engaged in separate tasks to which each was best fitted. In other words, being 'one flesh' did not deprive either of them of individuality or separate interests and activities."[4]

KINSHIP OF CHRIST AND MAN

If we are to follow the template of Adam and Eve, we read in Moses that each helped with their partner's duties. Eve labored in the field with Adam,[5] and Adam assisted in the nurturing and rearing of the children. Elder Marion G. Romney said, "In Latter-day Saint families the husband and wife must be one."[6]

Just as we discussed the special kinship that Christ feels with women and vice versa, Christ and men share a divine role as well. Christ provides for all of us, covering us with the protection of the Atonement. Every husband and father is expected to provide for and protect his family as well as he can, as he follows the commandments, adheres to his covenants, and honors his priesthood.

While some aspects of the roles of men and women converge or cross over, each must be in tune with the Spirit to know how to best serve in those roles. Both are called upon—and blessed—to protect the family and each other. While the wife may not be physically able to protect the husband or even the entire family, she can protect the sanctity of the home. She lives and nurtures in such a way that feelings of love, safety, and security can dwell within the heart of *each* family member. She can create the spiritual haven that each family member, including the husband, needs and craves, away from the world and its increasing harshness and evil influences.

THE FIRST DUTY OF A HUSBAND

As discussed earlier, the scriptural image of "cleaving" is similar to the idea of flesh cleaving to bone, of being so close that one is closely connected with the other. Each is different when separated but united in purpose.

In Hebrew, this phrase of Adam's ("bone of my bones and flesh of my flesh") indicates a very intimate, close, and unified relationship. So, far from indicating that Adam possesses Eve, this indicates an intimate and strengthening partnership between and for the two.

Husbands are to "love [their wives] with all [their hearts], and shalt cleave unto [them] and none else."[7] Our most important work is and will be within the walls of our homes.[8] Both spouses are to support each other in their respective duties and responsibilities,[9] of helping each other and their children qualify for eternal life. It is important to note that the scripture commands the husband to cleave to the wife and none else. This means she takes the preeminent place[10]—above parents, above children, above anyone except God.

DUTY OF A FATHER

D. Todd Christofferson taught:

> As a Church, we believe in fathers. We believe in "the ideal of the man who puts his family first." We believe that "by divine design, fathers are to preside over their families in love and righteousness and are responsible to provide the necessities of life and protection for their families." We believe that in their complementary family duties, "fathers and mothers are obligated to help one another as equal partners." We believe that far from being superfluous, fathers are *unique and irreplaceable*.
>
> Fatherhood is much more than a social construct or the product of evolution. The role of father is of divine origin, beginning with a Father in Heaven and, in this mortal sphere, with Father Adam. The perfect, divine expression of fatherhood is our Heavenly Father. His character and attributes include abundant goodness and perfect love. His work and glory are the development, happiness, and eternal life of His children.[11]

Christofferson continues as he counsels fathers: "Loving the mother of his children—and showing that love—are two of the best things a father can do for his children. This reaffirms and strengthens the marriage that is the foundation of their family life and security."

Speak words of comfort and kindness, courtesy, and respect. The greatest father to his children is the kindest husband to his wife. A great deal of security and safety that a child feels lies within the esteem that his or her father holds and treats the mother in.[12]

SUBMISSION—LISTENING TO COUNSEL OR PLEDGING OBEDIENCE?

The apocryphal manuscript of additional teachings of Jesus, found by Nicolas Notovitch in 1887, reads, "Be submissive toward your wife. Her love ennobles man, softens his hardened heart, tames the brute in him, and makes of him a lamb."[13]

For two righteous people, married in the new and everlasting covenant and faithfully keeping commandments and covenants, submitting[14] to one another is neither a punishment nor controversial. It becomes paramount in a healthy and happy relationship. Husband and wife are to heed each other's counsel, recognizing that their partner's vantage point is different from their own. We must remember as well that Paul was counseling the husbands on the sacred nature of their calling. Monte S. Nyman, et. al, wrote, "The marriage of a man and woman is a symbol of Jesus' relationship to the church."[15]

Ezra Taft Benson said, "Nothing except God Himself takes priority over your wife in your life—not work, not recreation, not hobbies. Your wife is your precious, eternal helpmate—your companion."[16]

Saving marriages takes faith, patience, and more than just a bit of time. Both spouses should be hopeful, believing, and enduring.[17] Dieter F. Uchtdorf said, "It requires you to be kind, envy not, seek not your own, not be easily provoked, think no evil, and rejoice in the truth. In other words, it requires charity, the pure love of Christ."[18]

Ultimately, successful relationships contain two people who submit fully to Heavenly Father and Jesus Christ, both heeding counsel and pledging obedience. With such a couple God is able to construct something holy.

ADAM'S RIB AND THE MASTER BUILDER

When the Lord takes the "rib" from Adam and makes a woman, the Hebrew word (for rib) used is *'tsela*. In all other instances in the Old Testament, this word is actually translated and used as "side,"[19] usually in the context of a tabernacle or temple construction. Only in these two verses in Genesis[20] is the word translated as "rib."

The Master Builder himself uses the "side" of *'adam* to create or "build" (*banah*) another human. Utilizing this translation for *'tsela* in this symbolic narrative better dramatizes a unity that man and woman are to strive for. It enhances the imagery of God creating two beings out of one. This brings more meaning to Adam's declaration of Eve as "bone of my bone and flesh of my flesh."[21]

Imagine the two symbolically creating a temple. A husband and father would do well to contemplate the full meaning of this imagery in his relationships.

In "The Apochryphon of John" it is recorded that Adam reacted with poetic delight when he first beheld Eve: "And he (Adam) saw the woman beside him. And in that moment the luminous Epinoia[22] appeared, and she lifted the veil which lay over his mind. And he became sober from the drunkenness of darkness. And he recognized his counter-image, and he said, 'This is indeed bone of my bones and flesh of my flesh.' Therefore the man will leave his father and his mother he will cleave to his wife and they will both be one flesh . . . and he will leave his father and his mother."[23] 'Adam—man—is never fully awake until his other equal half is created and united with him.

Jolen Edmunds Rockwood wrote, "*Bone* in Hebrew symbolizes power, and *flesh* weakness. 'Bone of my bones and flesh of my flesh'[24] thus become a ritual pledge to be bound in the best of circumstances (power) as well as the worst (weakness)."[25] We see in Adam's phrasing a familiar contemporary tome of "for better or for worse."

The image of a rib represents intimacy as well as identity, and we see this same expression in Genesis 2:24 when the two are declared "one flesh." Just as in the "cleave" discussion, the two—Adam and Eve—are to be inseparable companions. "What therefore God hath joined together, let not man put asunder."[26] It's not hard to imagine Adam reacting with delight when he was introduced to Eve because of the immediate closeness he felt with her.[27]

Nibley reiterated, "It is the clear declaration that man and woman were put on earth to stay together and have a family—*that is their first obligation and must supersede everything else.*"[28]

THE DIVINITY WITHIN FATHERHOOD

The perfect example that men can look to is their Heavenly Father. The role of fatherhood did not originate as a social experiment. It began with a Father in Heaven and continued with this earth's first mortal father, Adam.[29] Just as Heavenly Father's work and glory are to bring to pass His children's immortality (through required covenants that enable progression and eternal life), fathers are to emulate God's attributes, presiding in a way that provides *priesthood* protection. A father's role is to live in such a way that will allow the Spirit to thrive in the family, helping each family member feel safe to progress.[30]

We find in the scriptures a repeated emphasis on the parental obligation to teach one's children.[31] Elder D. Todd Christofferson taught, "The most essential of a father's work is to turn the hearts of his children to their Heavenly Father."[32]

Elder Christofferson continued:

> Far from being superfluous, fathers are unique and irreplaceable. . . . The Lord has said that "all children have claim upon their parents for their maintenance until they are of age."[33] Breadwinning is a consecrated activity. Providing for one's family, although it generally requires time away from the family, is not inconsistent with fatherhood—it is the essence of being a good father. 'Work and family are overlapping domains.'[34] This, of course, does not justify a man who neglects his family for his career or, at the other extreme, one who will not exert himself and is content to shift his responsibility to others.[35]

An ideal husband and father will emulate his Father in Heaven, who has never demeaned our Mother in Heaven. He feels and demonstrates perfect love to his children and wife.[36] This charge of protection they are to provide for families includes emotional and spiritual protection. A majority of that responsibility is to love and show love toward the mother of his children. The husband who exhibits these godly traits honors his priesthood. He will speak and act out of love and with a desire to bless his wife and family, not to dominate or dictate.

ENDNOTES

1. Uchtdorf, Dieter F. "In Praise of Those Who Save." The Church of Jesus Christ of Latter-day Saints, 2016. https://www.churchofjesuschrist.org/study/general-conference/2016/04/in-praise-of-those-who-save?lang=eng.

2. ChurchofJesusChrist.org/topics/family-proclamation?lang=eng.

3. Spencer W. Kimball, "Fundamental Principles to Ponder and Live," The Church of Jesus Christ of Latter-day Saints, Churchofjesuschrist.org/study/ensign/1978/11/fundamental-principles-to-ponder-and-live?lang=eng, accessed November 30, 2019.

4. Hugh Nibley, "Patriarchy and Matriarchy," *Old Testament and Related Studies*, vol. 1 in *The Collected Works of Hugh Nibley* (Salt Lake City: Deseret Book and Foundation for Ancient Research & Mormon Studies [FARMS]), 1986.

5. Moses 5:1

6. *Relief Society Magazine*, February 1968, 85–86.

7. Doctrine and Covenants 42:22

8. Harold B. Lee, "Love at Home," The Church of Jesus Christ of Latter Day Saints, ChurchofJesusChrist.org/manual/teachings-harold-b-lee/chapter-14?lang=eng#note1–, accessed November 12, 2019. (Press release for Mexico and Central America Area Conference 1972, 2.)

9. It is counterproductive to debate the importance of one parent over the other. Each is equipped with differing, as well as many of the same, qualities. However, each will have a different approach to these roles and responsibilities. A mother's influence is paramount in the early years, and the father contributes in greater and greater increments as the child grows to maturity. Both are necessary at all stages. In general, mothers prepare children to

live harmoniously within a family sphere and fathers prepare for the outside world. Once again, at differing levels and stages, and with different styles, both parents contribute and share with each other's duties and responsibilities. Both are vital. Serious consequences ensue with the removal or lack of contribution of either parent.

10. A great example of this is Lehi. When Sariah became worried about her sons (and was not just a little snarky with her husband), we read that Lehi did comfort her with his words (see 1 Nephi 5:4–6). He was the prophet, but he was also her husband and understood that this wasn't easy for her.

11. D. Todd Christofferson, "Fathers," The Church of Jesus Christ of Latter-day Saints, 2016, Churchofjesuschrist.org/study/general-conference/2016/04/fathers?lang=eng, emphasis added.

12. See Jacob 2:35

13. Alonzo L. Gaskill, in *The Lost Teachings of Jesus on the Sacred Place of Women* (Springville, UT: Cedar Fort Publishing and Media, 2014). quoting Nicolas Notovitch, *The Unknown Life of Jesus Christ—The Original Text of Nicolas Notovitch's 1887 Discovery.*

14. See also Ephesians 5:22–25.

15. Monte S. Nyman, Charles D. Tate, and Gary R. Whiting, "The Commandment to Be Perfect," in *The Book of Mormon: 3 Nephi 9–30, This Is My Gospel: Papers from the Eighth Annual Book of Mormon Symposium, 1993* (Salt Lake City, UT: Greg Kofford Books, 2008), 110.

16. Ezra Taft Benson, "To the Fathers in Israel," The Church of Jesus Christ of Latter-day Saints, churchofjesuschrist.org/study/general-conference/1987/10/to-the-fathers-in-israel?lang=eng.1, accessed December 1, 2019.

17. See Corinthians 13:7

18. Dieter F. Uchtdorf, "In Praise of Those Who Save," The Church of Jesus Christ of Latter-day Saints, 2016, ChurchofJesusChrist.org/general-conference/2016/04/in-praise-of-those-who-save?lang=eng.

19. George V. Wigram, in *The Englishman's Hebrew and Chaldee Concordance of the Old Testament: Numerically Coded to Strongs*

Exhaustive Concordance, 5th ed. (Grand Rapids, MI: Baker Book House, 1985), 1073–1074.

According to Jolene Edmunds Rockwood, "'Seal' refers to the side of a hill in 2 Samuel 16:13, but every other usage gives construction details for the tabernacle or temple.

20. Genesis 2:21–22

21. Moses 3:23, Genesis 2:23, Abraham 5:17

22. According to Laurence Caruana, *Epinoia* is a gnostic term/ name whose "main function is to awaken, or preserve hidden knowledge, as a means of rectifying ignorance and forgetfulness. . . . Epinoia appears in the story of Adam and Eve as an awakener to help Adam remember his true origins in the Upper Aeons. . . . Epinoia . . . was planted in Eve while she was still in Adam. Her role is to be an awakener: *"And he (the Spirit) sent a helper to Adam, luminous Epinoia which comes out of him, who is called Life. And she assists the whole creature, by toiling with him and by restoring him to his fullness and by teaching him about the descent of his seed (and) by teaching him about the way of ascent, (which is) the way he came down. And the luminous Epinoia was hidden in Adam, in order that the archons might not know her"* (Apocryphon of John), gnosticq.com/az.text/glos.af.html#Anchor-EPINOIA-30815

23. Robinson, James N., ed. "The Apocryphan of John," in *The Nag Hammadi Library* (New York, NY: Harper Collins), 1990, 118.

24. This phrase is used seven times in scripture (Genesis 29:14, 37:27; Judges 9:2; 2 Samuel 5:1, 19:12; 1 Chronicles 11:1; Isaiah 58:7), and each time it is meant to emphasize and affirm blood ties with relatives, not to suggest that one person was created physically from another. When used in a marriage ceremony, it is a declaration that the two are now bound as closely as if they came from the same parents (Shira Halevi, in *The Life Story of Adam and Havah: a New Targum of Genesis 1:26–5:5* [Aronson, 1997], 162–3).

25. Jolene Edmunds Rockwood, "The Redemption of Eve," in *Sisters in Spirit: Mormon Women in Historical and Cultural Perspective*, ed. Maureen Ursenbach. Beecher and Lavina Fielding Anderson (Urbana, I: University of Illinois Press, 1992), 12.

26. Mark 10:9

27. Genesis 2:23

28. Nibley, ibid., emphasis added.
29. Christofferson, ibid.
30. In his talk on "Fathers," Elder Christofferson articulated it this way: "His work and glory are the development, happiness, and eternal life of His children."
31. "And again, inasmuch as parents have children in Zion, or in any of her stakes which are organized, that teach them not to understand the doctrine of repentance, faith in Christ the Son of the living God, and of baptism and the gift of the Holy Ghost by the laying on of the hands, when eight years old, the sin be upon the heads of the parents. . . . And they shall also teach their children to pray, and to walk uprightly before the Lord (D&C 68:25–28).
32. Christofferson, ibid.
33. Doctrine and Covenants 83:4
34. David Blankenhorn, in *Fatherless America: Confronting Our Most Urgent Social Problem* (New York, NY: HarperPerennial, 1996), p. 113.
35. Christofferson, ibid.
36. Doctrine and Covenants 121:41–42

Chapter 13

THE PRIESTHOOD

Neither is the man without the woman,
neither the woman without the man,
in the Lord.

–1 Corinthians 11:11

WHAT IS THE PRIESTHOOD? [1]

Priesthood is the power of God, existing through the eternities, "without beginning of days or end of years."[2] It is through this authority and power that God is able to "bring to pass the immortality and eternal life of man"[3] along with the creation of the heavens and earth. It is the power that we will be resurrected by.[4]

The authority of the priesthood is given to man to act in God's name. Worthy priesthood holders are given authority to assist God by administering the saving ordinances of the gospel.[5] All of Heavenly Father's children—male or female—will be given the opportunity, whether in this life or the next, to qualify for blessings of priesthood ordinances.[6] It is through the priesthood power that we are able to be redeemed and exalted.

Latter-day Saint scholar Robert Millet defined the priesthood well when he said that it is "the power of God by which the worlds were made, by which all things are held in check in this and myriad universes, and the power by which human souls are regenerated, renewed, resurrected, redeemed, and glorified. In addition, the priesthood is the power and authority of god, delegated to man on earth, to act in all things for the salvation of men and women."[7]

The priesthood is not solely a male administration. It is God's power, designated in and with trust to men, to be used only to bless others. It allows recognition of ordinances by the Lord.[8]

Millet also writes, "Men are called to the priesthood to assist in the redemption of souls. They are called to preach and make available what Paul described as 'the ministry of reconciliation.'[9] They are called to bless lives—to lighten burdens, to strengthen the feeble knees and lift up the hands that hang down—just as their Master, the great High Priest, is called upon to do."[10]

Priesthood is the authority granted by God to man on earth, to act for Him and in His name, doing "what He would do if He were present."[11] For instance, with the restoration of the priesthood Joseph Smith was authorized to reorganize the Church of Jesus Christ, acting in His name, doing what Christ would do if He were present; for indeed the Church of Jesus Christ of Latter-day Saints is the Lord's Church, "governed by and through priesthood authority and priesthood keys."[12]

HISTORY OF WOMEN AND THE PRIESTHOOD

In the early days of the Church it was not uncommon for women to administer blessings of healing. In the 1880s, this included ritually washing another woman about to give birth.[13] This particular practice, as well as traditional "laying on of hands," was seen as a way for fellow sisters in Christ to minister to one who was in need. Many Relief Society sisters simply saw that doing so was an extension of their callings as personal ministers, aiding those who were sick, afflicted, and poor in spirit.

These women knew that their ability to bless and heal by "laying on of hands" was merely one of the many gifts of the Spirit that were available to followers, believers, and disciples of Christ, as taught in the New Testament. Joseph Smith himself noted, "It is no sin for any body to do it that has faith. . . . If the sisters should have faith to heal the sick, let all hold their tongues, and let every thing roll on."[14]

In 1883, Eliza Snow, General Relief Society President, explained that in these cases, women were administering by faith in the name of Jesus[15] and described it as their privilege and "imperative duty to apply them for the relief of human suffering."[16] The only requisite was that they be administered in "faith and humility." She and the other Relief Society sisters sincerely felt that God sanctioned such actions and granted them the power and healing that was requested at their hands.

In 1888, President Wilfred Woodruff confirmed that there was no wrongdoing in such a practice of "washing and anointing sisters who are approaching their confinement." Clarifying that it was *not an ordinance*, he further stated, "There is no impropriety in [such a practice]; but it should be understood that they do this, not as members of the priesthood, but as members of the Church, exercising faith for, and asking the blessings of the Lord upon, their sisters; just as they, and every member of the Church, might do for members of their families."[17]

By the early twentieth century this practice of ritual washing, as well as others that involved women giving blessings of healing the sick, was discontinued. The First Presidency instead encouraged members to call on the Elders as is directed in the New Testament (see James 5:14). Today only Melchizedek Priesthood holders administer to the sick, also referred to as *laying on of hands*.[18]

FEMALE PRIESTHOOD AUTHORITY

President Russell M. Nelson taught, "There is a difference between the authority of the priesthood and the power of the priesthood. Priesthood authority comes from ordination. Power comes from personal righteousness."[19]

While only male members of The Church of Jesus Christ of Latter-day Saints hold priesthood offices,[20] both male and female members officiate in sacred ordinances of the temple (with the temple president holding the keys). Covenant-keeping women are entitled to every blessing associated with the priesthood. This includes the power of the patriarchal order, entered into in the temple, to become goddesses, queens, and priestesses. Women also are given priesthood authority outside of the temple whenever they are set apart for a calling or to serve a mission.

The Latter-day Saint cultural narrative is shifting from referring to the priesthood as a sex or gender. Dallin H. Oaks said, "Priesthood power blesses all of us. Priesthood keys direct women as well as men, and priesthood ordinances and priesthood authority pertain to women as well as men."[21] Both men and women are given authority to perform certain things that are necessary—and just as binding—for salvation for their gospel brothers and sisters (as well as the rest of mankind). Since the Garden of Eden, worthiness and obedience have always been the prerequisite for any power, authority, or blessings.

Women lead in numerous organizations in the Church's congregations, including—but not limited to—praying, preaching, teaching, and proselyting. An obvious case in point is the Relief Society, "a divinely established appendage to the priesthood"[22] in which the women have the privilege of looking after the spiritual and physical welfare of people, both inside and outside of the Church.

President Dallin H. Oaks said, "We sometimes say that the Relief Society is a 'partner with the priesthood.' It would be more accurate to say that in the work of the Lord the Relief Society and the women of the Church are 'partners with *the holders* of the priesthood.'"[23]

AUTHORITY, ORDINATION, AND KEYS

Women are given priesthood authority to perform a specific priesthood function, such as when she is set apart to preach the gospel as a full-time missionary for the Church, or as an officer or teacher. President Oaks taught, "Whoever functions in an office or calling received from one who holds priesthood keys exercises priesthood authority in performing her or his assigned duties."[24]

Oaks also said:

In an address to the Relief Society, President Joseph Fielding Smith, then President of the Quorum of the Twelve Apostles, said this: " . . . A person may have authority given to him, or a sister to her, to do certain things in the Church that are binding and *absolutely necessary for our salvation*, such as the work that our sisters do in the House of the Lord. *They have authority given unto them to do some great and wonderful things, sacred unto the Lord, and binding just as thoroughly as are the blessings that are given by the men who hold the Priesthood.*"

In that notable address, President Smith said again and again that women have been given authority. To the women he said, "You can speak with authority, because the Lord has placed authority upon you. . . . The work which they [Relief Society] do is done by divine authority." (emphasis added)

The scriptures indicate that male *ordination* of the priesthood is the pattern the Church is to follow.[25] For instance, when Christ organized His church, He called men to serve as His Apostles. While both men and women were and can be *disciples and witnesses*,[26] only males are called as *special* witnesses. But this in no ways negates a righteous woman's ability to "speak with the power and authority of God."[27]

Both men and women are given priesthood *authority*.[28] Both sexes are endowed and clothed with priesthood vestments and power in the temple, thus able to work on behalf of their ancestors of their respective gender. The Lord recognizes the divine authority of both men and women as they officiate in the temple.[29]

There are delegated divisions within the priesthood: "deacon, teacher, priest, elder, high priest, patriarch, seventy, and Apostle—always come by *ordination*."[30] Other callings, including serving in a presidency (whether it be sisters or brothers) are received by *setting apart*.[31] While both male and female members are set apart and hold offices including in auxiliary presidencies, only male ordained members receive keys.[32]

Jesus Christ holds all the priesthood keys. Acts under the direction of the priesthood must be done in a proper way, place, and time. Whoever has the *keys* has the authority from Heavenly Father to direct the use of the priesthood in official labors on the earth. Only the prophet of God (and president of The Church of Jesus Christ of Latter-day Saints) is authorized to hold all of the keys at once. He has the authority to delegate certain keys and the labors associated. The person who holds the keys to a specific organization is authorized to direct it, but does not hold any more priesthood than the other men in that organization or quorum.[33]

Other organizations within the Church—such as Relief Society, Primary, Young Men and Young Women, and Sunday School—are considered auxiliaries *to* the priesthood.

THE PRIESTHOOD AND THE FAMILY

While church positions and callings are temporary, the family unit and relationships are permanent. The government differs in the Church and the family. The Church's government is hierarchical, while the home's government is patriarchal, meaning that it is *established* through the new and everlasting covenant of marriage, the patriarchal *order*.

Dallin H. Oaks explains the different and similar ways the priesthood functions in the home and in the Church:[34] "The family is dependent upon the Church for doctrine, ordinances, and priesthood keys. The Church provides the teachings, authority, and ordinances necessary to perpetuate family relationships to the eternities."

As the family is dependent upon the Church, the Church is dependent upon the strength of the family, and the priesthood is used in both the home and the Church. Of all the units in the Church, the family is the most important.

The difference in the exercise of the priesthood between the family and Church, Oaks says, are the *keys*:

> All priesthood authority *in the Church* functions under the direction of the one who holds the appropriate priesthood keys. . . . In contrast, the authority that presides *in the family* . . . functions in family matters without the need to get authorization from anyone holding priesthood keys. This family authority includes directing the activities of the family, family

meetings like family home evenings, family prayer, teaching the gospel, and counseling and disciplining family members. It also includes ordained fathers giving priesthood blessings.

However, priesthood keys are necessary to authorize the ordaining or setting apart of family members. This is because *the organization the Lord has made responsible for the performance and recording of priesthood ordinances is the Church, not the family.*[34]

As we examine the duties of family authority as stated above, it is recognized that in a contemporary family both men and women exercise all of these duties (save for giving priesthood blessings, which are reserved for righteous, ordained fathers).

WHY IS THE PRIESTHOOD ORDINATION ONLY FOR MEN? [35]

M. Russell Ballard, quoting President Gordon B. Hinckley, explained, "'It was the Lord,' not man, 'who designated that men in His Church should hold the priesthood' and who endowed women with 'capabilities to round out this great and marvelous organization, which is the Church and kingdom of God.' The Lord has not revealed why He has organized His Church as He has."[36]

Hinckley said to women, "He who is our Eternal Father has blessed you with miraculous powers of mind and body. He never intended that you should be less than the crowning glory of His creations."[37]

Elder Ballard said, "We know [priesthood ordination] is not because men are inherently more righteous or more faithful than women, because that simply is not true."[38] Both men and women, no matter how they are functioning within the priesthood, are to have patience, long-suffering,[39] and serve with an eye single to the glory of God.[40]

Both men and women have been promised that if they are obedient, they will become joint heirs with Christ.[41] This blessing is not reserved just for men ordained to the priesthood.

But perhaps we are asking the wrong question. Perhaps the question should be why are men *required* to be ordained and women are not? Neither male nor female are able to receive a fulness of the priesthood in the temple, nor exaltation, without the complementary gender. This is God's church, authority, and direction originating from Him. Revelation has not been received concerning the ordination of women.[42]

Whatever the reason, we can trust that God, as no respecter of persons, has His daughters forefront in His mind, with all things and intentions for their glory.

ENDNOTES

1. "Ultimately, the term 'priesthood,' in the sense of a generic authority from God, came to replace the term 'holy order,' while the term 'order' continues to be used, but usually in the sense of the major divisions (orders) or Aaronic, Patriarchal, and Melchizedek priesthood . . . [in] the Book of Mormon . . . 'holy order' was the standard term used to denote authority from God" (John A. Tvedtness, "The Holy Order," Book of Mormon Research, bookofmormonresearch.org/the-holy-order, accessed October 15, 2018).

2. Joseph Smith and Joseph Fielding Smith, in *Teachings of the Prophet Joseph Smith*, vol. 1 (American Fork, UT: Covenant Communications, 2005), 57.

3. Moses 1:39

4. Dallin H. Oaks, "The Keys and Authority of the Priesthood," The Church of Jesus Christ of Latter-day Saints, April 2014, churchofjesuschrist.org/study/general-conference/2014/04/the-keys-and-authority-of-the-priesthood?lang=eng&_r=1.
    See also Boyd K. Packer, "Priesthood Power in the Home" (worldwide leadership training meeting, February 2012).

5. Saving ordinances are essential to our exaltation. "They include baptism, confirmation, ordination to the Melchizedek Priesthood (for men), the temple endowment, and the marriage sealing" (ChurchofJesusChrist.org/topics/ordinances?lang=eng).

6. ChurchofJesusChrist.org/youth/learn/ap/priesthood-keys/what?lang=eng

7. Robert L. Millet, "Restoring the Patriarchal Order," GospeLink.com, gospelink.com/library/document/30117?highlight=1, accessed December 3, 2019.

8. ChurchofJesusChrist.org/manual/gospel-principles/chapter-13–the-priesthood?lang=eng.

9. 2 Corinthians 5:18

10. Robert L. Millet, "The Holy Order of God," in *The Book of Mormon: Alma, the Testimony of the Word*, ed. Monte S. Nyman and Charles D. Tate (Provo, UT: Brigham Young University Religious Studies Center, 1992), 61–68.

11. Boyd K. Packer, "What Every Elder Should Know—and Every Sister as Well: A Primer on Principles of Priesthood Government," churchofjesuschrist.org/study/ensign/1993/02/what-every-elder-should-know-and-every-sister-as-well-a-primer-on-principles-of-priesthood-government?lang=eng, accessed December 3, 2019. JST, Genesis 14:28–31

12. M. Russell Ballard, "Men and Women and Priesthood Power," The Church of Jesus Christ of Latter-day Saints, September 2014, churchofjesuschrist.org/study/ensign/2014/09/men-and-women-and-priesthood-power?lang=eng.
    Handbook 2: Administering the Church (2010), 2.1.1. says the following: "'Priesthood keys are the authority God has given to priesthood leaders to direct, control, and govern the use of His priesthood on earth. The exercise of priesthood authority is governed by those who hold its keys (see Doctrine and Covenants 65:2; 81:2; 124:123) . . . [and] who have the right to preside over and direct the Church within a jurisdiction'" (churchofjesuschrist.org/bc/content/shared/content/english/pdf/language-materials/08702_eng.pdf?lang=eng).

13. This particular tradition is not to be confused with the washing and anointing ordinance that takes place in the temple.

14. Eliza R. Snow, "Nauvoo Relief Society Minute Book, Page 36," *Joseph Smith Papers*, josephsmithpapers.org/paper-summary/nauvoo-relief-society-minute-book/33, accessed December 3, 2019.

15. Ibid., Mark 16:17–18.

16. Jill Mulvay Derr et al., in *The First Fifty Years of Relief Society: Key Documents in Latter-Day Saint Women's History* (Salt Lake City, UT: The Church Historian's Press, 2016), 515–16.

17. Ibid., 541–42.
    See also Danielle B. Wagner, "Mormon Women Giving Blessings: Everything You Need to Know," *LDS Living*, December

11, 2018, ldsliving.com/Women-Giving-Blessings-in-the-Early-Days-of-the-Church/s/81418/?utm_source=ldsliving&utm_medium=sidebar&utm_campaign=related.

18. *Handbook 2:Administering the Church*, 20.6.1.

19. Russell M. Nelson et al., "Priesthood," The Church of Jesus Christ of Latter-day Saints, ChurchofJesusChrist.org/topics/priesthood?lang=eng, accessed December 3, 2019.

20. "First Presidency Statement," Office of the First Presidency, June 28, 2018, ChurchofJesusChrist.org/prophets-and-apostles/june-first-presidency-statement?lang=eng.

21. Oaks, ibid.

22. Ibid.

23. Ibid., footnote 11.

24. Ibid.

25. See for instance: Numbers 3:3, 10; Abraham 1:3, 26, 31; Doctrine and Covenants 20:38, 48–50, 56, 60, 64, 76, 78.

26. Mary was the first witness of the resurrected Christ.

27. Russell M. Nelson, "A Plea to My Sisters," The Church of Jesus Christ of Latter-day Saints, October 2015, ChurchofJesusChrist.org/general-conference/2015/10/a-plea-to-my-sisters?lang=eng.

28. Oaks, ibid.

29. Dallin H. Oaks and Joseph Fielding Smith, "The Relief Society and the Church," The Church of Jesus Christ of Latter-day Saints, ChurchofJesusChrist.org/general-conference/1992/04/the-relief-society-and-the-church?lang=eng, accessed November 15, 2019. (Joseph Fielding Smith, October 1958 LDS General conference, as quoted by Dallin H. Oaks).

30. Boyd K. Packer, "What Every Elder Should Know—and Every Sister as Well: A Primer on Principles of Priesthood Government," The Church of Jesus Christ of Latter-day Saints, ChurchofJesusChrist.org/ensign/1993/02/what-every-elder-should-know-and-every-sister-as-well-a-primer-on-principles-of-priesthood-government?lang=eng, accessed December 7, 2019, emphasis added.

31. Ibid. "There are two ways authority is conferred in the Church: by ordination and by setting apart. Offices in the priesthood . . . always come by ordination. The keys of presidency and the authority to act in callings in the priesthood are received by setting apart. . . . There are many "set apart" offices in the Church in

both the priesthood and the auxiliary organizations. Some duties are inherent in the priesthood, and one need not be set apart to do them. Visiting the homes of members . . . is an example.

"Because women are not ordained to the priesthood, when sisters are set apart to offices, including the office of president in an auxiliary, they receive *authority, responsibility, and blessings connected* with the office, but they do not receive keys" (emphasis added).

For those not familiar with the Church's practices the act of ordination, blessings, and setting apart visually look the same. At least two men ordained to the priesthood place their hands on the recipient's head. What changes is the wording and depending on the nature of the act the degree of priesthood. More info can be found at ChurchofJesusChrist.org/topics?lang=eng.

32. "The keys of the priesthood are the right to preside and direct the affairs of the Church within a jurisdiction. Jesus Christ holds all the keys of the priesthood pertaining to His Church. He has conferred upon each of His Apostles all the keys that pertain to the kingdom of God on earth. The senior living Apostle, the President of the Church, is the only person on earth authorized to exercise all priesthood keys" (ChurchofJesusChrist.org under Gospel Topics, Priesthood, ChurchofJesusChrist.org/topics/priesthood?lang=eng).

33. Joseph F. Smith, *Teachings of Presidents of the Church: Joseph F. Smith* (Salt Lake City, UT: The Church of Jesus Christ of Latter-day Saints, 1998), 141.

34. Dallin H. Oaks, "Priesthood Authority in the Family and the Church," The Church of Jesus Christ of Latter-day Saints, October 2005, ChurchofJesusChrist.org/general-conference/2005/10/priesthood-authority-in-the-family-and-the-church?lang=eng, emphasis added.

35. Lest we forget there have been times in history that the priesthood was for only a select group, we read in the Old Testament that only men of the tribe of Lehi were ordained to the priesthood.

36. M. Russell Ballard, "Men and Women and Priesthood Power," The Church of Jesus Christ of Latter-day Saints, September 2014, ChurchofJesusChrist.org/ensign/2014/09/men-and-women-and-priesthood-power?lang=eng.

37. Gordon B. Hinckley, "Stand Strong against the Wiles of the World," The Church of Jesus Christ of Latter-day Saints, churchofjesuschrist.org/study/ensign/1995/11/stand-strong-against-the-wiles-of-the-world?lang=eng, accessed December 7, 2019.

38. M. Russell Ballard, *When Thou Art Converted: Continuing Our Search for Happiness* (Salt Lake City, UT: Deseret Book, 2001), gospelink.com/library/document/19676.

39. Alma 7:23

40. Doctrine and Covenants 82:19

41. Romans 8:16–17

42. For some, the frustration and pain of not receiving ordination into the priesthood because of their gender is real. Some wonder if they will be able to enjoy the same blessings and value they see in their male counterparts. But for those that live up to their responsibilities, obligations, and covenants that are required of them in this life, Henry B. Eyring promised that all have been promised eternal arrangements that "will be more wonderful than you can imagine" (Henry B. Eyring, "The Hope of Eternal Family Love," The Church of Jesus Christ of Latter-day Saints, August 2016, churchofjesuschrist.org/study/ensign/2016/08/the-hope-of-eternal-family-love?lang=eng).

Chapter 14

THE PATRIARCHAL ORDER

*The highest order of the Melchizedek Priesthood is patriarchal authority. The order was divinely established with father Adam **and** mother Eve. They are the fount and progenitors of all living, and **they will appear** at the culmination of earth's history **at the head of the whole sealed family of the redeemed**.*[1]

—Lynn A. McKinlay

CLEARING UP THE CONFUSION: ORDER VERSUS THEOCRACY

In the Latter-day Saint mind, there is often confusion about what constitutes the patriarchal order. It helps to understand modern revelation and Old Testament culture.

Ezra Taft Benson explained, "The order of priesthood spoken of in the scriptures is sometimes referred to as the patriarchal order because it [the priesthood] came down from father to son.[2] But this order is otherwise described in modern revelation as *an order of family government where a man and woman enter into a covenant with God—just as did Adam and Eve—to be sealed for eternity, to*

107

have posterity, and to do the will and work of God throughout their mortality."[3]

"'All of the ancient patriarchs were high priests,'" Joseph Fielding Smith explained, 'but the direction of the Church in those days was by patriarchs'[4]. . . . This special designation of the chief spiritual officer of the Church has reference to the *administrative position which he holds rather than to the office to which he is ordained in the priesthood.*"[5]

In just the last twenty years we have witnessed a great deal of negativity toward the subject of *patriarchy*. It has often been associated with male chauvinism, abuse, and repression. However, there is a difference between patriarchal *order* and patriarchal *theocracy*.

We see examples of cultures living in a *patriarchal theocracy* in Old Testament times, when there was little to no separation between church and state. Presiding patriarchs, such as Adam, Enos, Jared, and Noah presided over and governed their posterity and members of God's earthly kingdom, called as high priests and presiding patriarchs.

The portion of priesthood required to seal marriages for time and eternity, to establish the *patriarchal order*, was present during Christ's ministry. While much has been removed from the scriptures, there are New Testament apocryphal writings called the "forty-day literature" that teach of sacred washings, holy garments, and sacred marriages.[6] But after the crucifixion of Christ and the death of the Apostles, these keys were taken. So, for the next seventeen centuries, both the priesthood and the beauty and partnership of eternal marriage were misunderstood and forgotten.

PRIESTHOOD RESTORED

In April of 1836, the keys to gather Israel (missionary work) were restored to Joseph Smith. Later, Elias returned the keys necessary to restore the true patriarchal order and its power to organize eternal families. These keys that open the blessings of the temple are the grand purpose for all the other covenants, principles, and ordinances. The keys restored by Moses, Elias, and Elijah and the respective ordinances related to those keys are referred to as the "capstone blessings of the gospel."[7]

This allows couples to enter into the patriarchal order in the holy temple, to be sealed for eternity. It "is here called an 'order of the priesthood.' A necessary step to the establishment of an eternal family, in which *both husband and wife hold priesthood responsibility for their posterity.*"[8]

The patriarchal order is also referred to as the new and everlasting covenant,[9] or Abrahamic covenant. Doctrine and Covenants 132:63 speaks of "eternal lives," referring to the continuation of the family in eternity, creating spirit children just as our Heavenly Parents created us. The patriarchal order is the foundation, the basis, and the means of an eternal family organization.

The patriarchal order is not an order subscribing the husband to preside or rule in the home *alone*. The strong cultural undertones have confused this for many people. But as the gospel is continually in a state of restoration with more and more concepts being clarified, so are the roles of men and women and their duties, rights, and obligations within this order.

Men presiding, in the context of the home, refers to the use of priesthood in the home. Lynn A. McKinlay explained, "To Latter-day Saints, the patriarchal order of the priesthood is the organizing power and principle of celestial family life. It is the ultimate and ideal form of government. . . . The order was divinely established with father Adam and mother Eve. They are the fount and progenitors of all living, and they will appear at the culmination of earth's history at the head of the whole sealed family of the redeemed. The promises given to Abraham and Sarah pertain to this same order."[10]

Two righteous individuals enter into the highest order of the Melchizedek Priesthood, blessings to be given to both husbands and wives *together*. As Valerie Cassler articulated, "We become a faith community of priests and priestesses,[11] then, and when united in the new and everlasting covenant of marriage, men and women together hold the fullness of the Priesthood, its capital 'P' signifying more than the male-only priesthood."[12]

THE PATRIARCHAL ORDER IS A HEAVENLY FAMILY ORDER

In our premortal life, we existed in a heavenly family consisting of a Heavenly Father, Heavenly Mother, and spirit siblings. All of us were presided over by both Heavenly Father *and* Mother—both perfect and governing with love, kindness, and gentle persuasion. We learned early on that because of free agency, our greatest joys and sorrows occur within a family unit, both premortal and earthly. We, and our Heavenly Parents, lost one-third of our family through unrighteous choices. (But despite the risks, following this template brings us the most joy.)

Lynn McKinlay wrote, "Thus united, [parents] work in love, faith, and harmony for the glorification of their family. If they are not united in obedient love, if they are not one, they are not of the Lord. Eventually, through this Order, families will be linked in indissoluble bonds all the way back to the first parents, and all the way forward to the last child born into this world. This priesthood order will be both the means and the end of reconciliation, redemption, peace, joy, and eternal life."[13]

With modern revelation, we learn that this order, a template established and followed by God and taught to Father Adam and Mother Eve, is nothing less than a family government patterned after a heavenly one, a divine one. It is, as Ezra T. Benson said, "an order of family government where a man and woman enter into a covenant with God—just as did Adam and Eve—to be sealed for eternity, to have posterity, and to do the will and work of God throughout their mortality."[14]

The most important service that any man or woman will perform will be within their family. We bless our posterity[15] when we enter into the Holy Order of God or patriarchal order.

THE FAMILY GOVERNMENT

Just as it is crucial for our testimonies and salvation to have a correct understanding of Heavenly Father, Heavenly Mother, and Jesus Christ, it is also important for men and women to have a correct understanding of how to function appropriately in a family government patterned after a heavenly one.

There has been a misunderstanding about the phrase "patriarchal order" in that some individuals and cultures have mistaken it for patriarchal (male only) leadership. While we do have patriarchs,[16] the patriarchal order is the *fulness of the Melchizedek priesthood* and can only be entered into by both the man *and* woman. In the family government there cannot be patriarchs without matriarchs, fathers without mothers.[17] Both share the blessings of the priesthood and minister in the affairs of the family government.[18]

Dean L. Larsen explained, "The patriarchal system provides a basis for government in the kingdom of God. It places parents in a position of accountability for their own direct family, and it links these family kingdoms in a patriarchal order that lends cohesiveness to the greater kingdom of God of which they are a part. The patriarchal order has no relevance in the eternal worlds except for those husbands and wives and families who have entered into the covenant of eternal marriage."[19]

We do know that both Adam and Eve called upon the name of the Lord,[20] with Eve serving "in matriarchal partnership with the patriarchal priesthood."[21] They both presided over their posterity, teaching the gospel as intelligent and equal partners. Often God made His will known not through the patriarch but through the matriarch.[22] In some cases, God even directed that the patriarch heed and hearken to the Great Matriarch.[23]

THE PATRIARCHAL ORDER IS A PARTNERSHIP—HUSBAND AND WIFE PRESIDING OVER A FAMILY

Both men *and* women enter into this holy order of the Son of God, and it can only be so in order to "one day see the face of God and live."[24] However, women are not under the same obligation of priesthood ordination before entering into the patriarchal order, but just as with their male counterparts, celestial marriage is a requirement for women to enter into the heavenly church.

Celestial marriage is labeled as the patriarchal order, not to designate the male as "the one in charge," but because it requires priesthood power to make the sealing effective, valid, and binding. It's helpful to envision two churches: our earthly church and the heavenly church (also called the Church of the Firstborn). The entrance requirement into the earthly church is baptism. The entrance requirement into the Church of the Firstborn is celestial marriage. It is this heavenly church where the family unit continues into the eternities.[25]

Brethren who have received the Melchizedek Priesthood covenant to "live by every word that proceedeth forth from the mouth of God."[26] They also covenant "to marry for time and all eternity in the patriarchal order,"[27] living and serving as Jesus Christ did.

James Harper magnificently wrote, "What we can conclude, then, particularly from what we know of the relationship between Adam and Eve, is that the executive council of husband and wife together is extremely important in the organization of families. Husbands and wives should counsel together in decisions related to communication and activities in the family, rearing and disciplining of children, food storage and other aspects of family welfare, finances, work and career decisions, family work responsibilities, housekeeping tasks, recreation, and all other decisions that affect their bond with each other."[28]

What a grand design and powerful plan to have a partner in our mission as parents!

ENDNOTES

1. Lynn A. McKinlay, "Patriarchal Order of the Priesthood," *The Encyclopedia of Mormonism*, 2011, eom.byu.edu/index.php/Patriarchal_Order_of_the_Priesthood, emphasis added.
2. Doctrine and Covenants 107:40–42; Abraham 1:2–3
3. Ezra Taft Benson, "What I Hope You Will Teach Your Children about the Temple," The Church of Jesus Christ of Latter-day Saints, ChurchofJesusChrist.org/ensign/1985/08/what-i-hope-you-will-teach-your-children-about-the-temple?-lang=eng, accessed December 7, 2019, emphasis added.
4. Joseph Fielding Smith, *Doctrines of Salvation*, 3 Volumes (Salt Lake City: Bookcraft, 1998), 3:104.

5. Bruce R. McConkie, *Mormon Doctrine*, 2nd ed. (Salt Lake City: Bookcraft, 1966), rsc.byu.edu/archived/5–holy-order-god. As quoted in Robert L. Millet, "The Holy Order of God," in *The Book of Mormon: Alma, The Testimony of the Word*, eds. Monte S. Nyman and Charles D. Tate Jr., (Provo, Utah: Religious Studies Center, Brigham Young University, 1992), 61–68, emphasis added..

6. Hugh Nibley, *Mormonism and Early Christianity*, ed. Todd M. Compton and Stephen D. Ricks (Salt Lake City: Deseret Book and FARMS, 1987), 10–44.

7. Robert L. Millet, "Restoring the Patriarchal Order," GospeLink.com, gospelink.com/library/document/30117?highlight=1, accessed December 3, 2019. See also Doctrine and Covenants 110:11–16.

8. John A. Tvedtnes, "The Patriarchal Order of Priesthood," *Meridian Magazine*, April 9, 2005, latterdaysaintmag.com/article-1–201/, emphasis added.

   "Children, male or female, born to such a union are born in this covenant. And they become legal heirs to all the priesthood blessings, privileges, and responsibilities of that covenant just as the sons of Aaron did in his day. This is contingent, as it was in that period of time, on their later being vested with those priestly identities in the temple. This makes such a birth, to a child born in the covenant, equivalent to a priesthood ordinance for it bestows upon the covenant woman's posterity a birthright that is both essential and otherwise attainable only through the sealing power of the priesthood.

   A child not so born can turn to someone with this sealing power to receive this blessing and birthright through a priesthood ordinance in the temple.

   "Giving birth may be one way that covenant women participate in the priesthood power of binding on earth what shall be bound in heaven, acting in the earth for the salvation of the human family" (Wendy Ulrich, PhD, "What I hope we will teach our daughters [and sons] about the priesthood," FAIRMormon Conference, Aug. 2014).

9. Doctrine and Covenants 131:1–4

10. Lynn A. McKinlay, "Patriarchal Order of the Priesthood," *Encyclopedia of Mormonism,* 4 vols. (New York: Macmillan Publishing Company, 1992).

11. squaretwo.org/Sq2ArticleCasslerOaksBallardDew.html
In the temple where faithful, covenant keeping people are anointed to become kings and queens, priests and priestesses to God. See John A. Tvedtnes, "The Patriarchal Order of Priesthood," *Meridian Magazine*, April 9, 2005, latterdaysaintmag.com/article-1–201/. See also Doctrine and Covenants 76:56.

12. Valerie Hudson Cassler, "Yard Work in the Kingdom of God: On False Conceptions about LDS Women," *Meridian Magazine*, July 21, 2014, latterdaysaintmag.com/article-1–14640–2/.

13. Lynn A. McKinlay, "Patriarchal Order of the Priesthood," *Encyclopedia of Mormonism*, 4 vols. (New York: Macmillan Publishing Company, 1992).

14. Moses 6:67; Ezra T. Benson, "What I Hope You Will Teach Your Children about the Temple," *Ensign,* August 1985.

15. Doctrine and Covenants 107:40–42

16. Such as the calling of patriarch

17. 1 Corinthians 11:11. The author, of course, is not referring to single-parent households. While the ideal is a two-parent system, it is recognized that there are several very faithful single-parent Christian households that succeed with God as their partner. This discussion is about the family government plan intended to follow the heavenly template.

18. James E. Talmage, *Young Woman's Journal 25* (Oct. 1914): 602–603.

19. Dean L. Larsen, "Marriage and the Patriarchal Order," *Ensign*, September 1982, ChurchofJesusChrist.org/ensign/1982/09/marriage-and-the-patriarchal-order?lang=eng

20. Moses 5:1–8

21. Russell M. Nelson, *The Power within Us* (Salt Lake City, UT: Deseret Book, 1988), 109.

22. See for instance: Sarai, Genesis 16:1–2; Rebekah, Genesis 25:23.

23. Genesis 21:12
God has directed men through the ages to listen and follow the counsel of their wives (see Genesis 16:1–2).
"And God said unto Abraham . . . In all that Sarah hath said unto thee, hearken unto her voice" (Genesis 21:12).

24. Doctrine and Covenants 84:19–22

25. Bruce R. McConkie, in *A New Witness for the Articles of Faith* (Salt Lake City, UT: Deseret Book, 1985), 337.

McConkie also wrote, "His eternal patriarchal order, an order that prevails in the highest heaven of the celestial world, an order that assures its members of eternal increase, or in other words of spirit children in the resurrection" (Bruce R. McConkie, "The Doctrine of the Priesthood," *Ensign*, May 1982, 32–34). See also Doctrine and Covenants 131:1–4

26. Doctrine and Covenants 84:44
27. McConkie, Ibid.
28. James M. Harper, "'A Man . . . Shall Cleave unto His Wife': Marriage and Family Advice from the Old Testament," Church of Jesus Christ, churchofjesuschrist.org/study/ensign/1990/01/a-man-shall-cleave-unto-his-wife-marriage-and-family-advice-from-the-old-testament?lang=eng, accessed December 7, 2019.

Chapter 15

HEAVENLY MOTHER

I had learned to call thee Father,
Thru thy Spirit from on high, But,

Until the key of knowledge Was
restored, I knew not why. In the

Heav'ns are parents single? No, the
thought makes reason stare! Truth

Is reason; truth eternal Tells me I've a
mother there.

—Eliza R. Snow

SCRIPTURAL EVIDENCE

Various religions around the world share the image of God as our Father and us as His children. Some accept this teaching as literal, and others see it only as a metaphor. Members of The Church of Jesus Christ of Latter-day Saints view various scriptures literally,[1] interpreting passages that speak of our potential to become like God. When Adam and Eve partook of the fruit, this began the necessary process of progressing to becoming like our Heavenly parents.[2]

117

Elder Dallin H. Oaks has acknowledged, "Our theology begins with heavenly parents. Our highest aspiration is to be like them."[3] In some respects, this is a very unique and progressive theology. There seems to be a collective yearning for female divinity. Church members, while comfortable with the idea of a heavenly mother, seem unsure of where this idea originated, and accept the cultural premise that there are few—if any—scriptures that speak directly of a heavenly mother. Despite popular belief, the idea of the divine feminine *is* evidenced in scripture.

In the book of Abraham, we read of *Shinehah*[4] the sun. This is a Hebrew word that (later on) came to mean "the presence of God." What is most interesting is that this Hebrew word is in feminine form, referring to the presence of the feminine form of God. Whenever a feminine form is used, especially in scripture, there is a context of a gentler, kinder, and nurturing quality.[5]

Genesis 1:26 reads, "Let *us* make man in *our* image after our likeness" (emphasis added). The plural account includes Jesus Christ and God the Father. Joseph Fielding Smith and other prophets in this dispensation agree that it implies that females (including goddesses) were involved in the planning and execution of the Creation—both the earth and of mankind. "Is it not feasible to believe that female spirits were created in the image of a 'Mother in Heaven?'" said Joseph Fielding Smith.[6]

EARLY CHURCH DOCTRINE

The earliest written references to this distinctive doctrine of a heavenly mother[7] do not surface until after 1844. The most famous is from a poem by Eliza R. Snow that now serves as text for the hymn "O My Father"[8] in which Wilford Woodruff declared it as revelation.[9] In 1909 the First Presidency taught in the article "The Origin of Man" that "all men and women are in the similitude of the universal Father and Mother, and are literally the sons and daughters of Deity."[10]

Many prophets and apostles over the ages have taught about a divine mother sitting side by side with a divine father, working together for the salvation of all of their earthly family.[11] The early church leaders, including Joseph Smith, Brigham Young, Heber C. Kimball, and Erastus Snow spoke frequently and freely about the existence of a Mother in Heaven, reigning and ruling equally, side by side, with Heavenly Father.[12]

James E. Talmage, in the context of discussing women's equal rights in the later years of the nineteenth century, spoke of how Heavenly Mother, along with all women, are just as essential to "carrying out God's purposes in respect to mankind."[13]

The overall church culture is moving away from a subculture of hesitating to speak directly about Mother in Heaven. The reality is that a divine pattern has been established by heavenly parents and revealed in scriptures and modern revelation.

Church members believe in the spiritual as well as physical parentage of all humanity[14] with the foundational logic of offspring needing both a mother and a father. Because of this belief, it is not difficult to visualize a heavenly mother like Heavenly Father in "glory, perfection, compassion, wisdom, and holiness."[15]

THE DIVINE FEMININE

Latter-day Saint doctrine affirms that all of us, regardless of gender, have always existed as intelligences. We had distinct and unique personalities; this was our core being. We were given the opportunity to follow an exalted path that was offered by our first parents—Heavenly Father and Heavenly Mother. We identified and defined ourselves with a specific gender, that of male or female, as an essential part of our core being, a "stewardship," if you will, of present and future roles and responsibilities.

Females have roles and privileges that, as Sharon Eubank so eloquently stated, "have to do with binding, connecting, bridging, gluing," suggesting that these words are a reflection of the Divine or Eternal Feminine.[16]

What, then, can we within a church of mostly male hierarchy, offer women of this world? The First Vision occurred during a time when women's rights, as we experience them today, were not even visualized yet. And yet, the leadership of the early church was surprisingly feministic, encouraging their families to follow suit.

For instance, Susa Young Gates (second daughter of Brigham Young's twenty-second wife), was an active Latter-day Saint and a staunch women's rights activist. She wrote a stirring essay about the freedom and promises now offered to women because of the First Vision.

> Therefore, the [First] Vision held the bright promise of equality and freedom for women. The divine Mother, side by side with the divine Father, the equal sharing of equal rights, privileges and responsibilities, in heaven and on earth, all this was foreshadowed in that startling announcement of the Son: "They were all wrong! They draw near to me with their lips, but their hearts are far from me!" In an age-long darkness and apostasy, woman had been shackled because of her very virtue, tender sympathy, and patient desire for peace. . . . Man had held woman by the wrist, had controlled her religiously, financially, and civilly. . . .
>
> What [did] the Vision [mean] to woman? It meant in civil, religious, social and finally, financial matters, the right of choice; it meant woman's free agency, the liberation of her long-chained will and purpose.[17]

Our very purpose, eternal progression, and growth is inextricably tied to family units and gender roles within the kingdom of God. According to the Family Proclamation, "gender is an essential characteristic of individual premortal, mortal, and eternal identity and purpose."

This earth is not our final resting place, nor our last and only home. It is "a training ground for souls learning to become like a divine Mother and Father. It holds that the creation, the loving, and the raising of new life are among the most essential human experiences to that end."[18] As husband and wife walk through life together, making sacrifices for each other and for the family they raise, those experiences help prepare them for eternal parentage, as long as it is coupled with obedience to God's commandments and keeping covenants made in the temple.

We express gratitude a Mother in Heaven for her "crucial role in fulfilling the purposes of eternity."[19]

UNDERSTANDING HER DIVINITY

Some scholars have made claim that Latter-day Saints have acknowledged "her existence only, without delving further into her character or roles, or portray her as merely a silent, Victorian-type housewife valued only for her ability to reproduce."[20]

Author Robert A. Rees wrote that "what we are left with is an image of our Heavenly Mother staying at home having billions of children while the men—the Father and his sons—go off to create worlds, spin galaxies, take business trips to outer space. She is happy, it would seem, to let them have all the recognition, all the glory."[21] However, Church leaders, including General Authorities, are making mention of *both* Heavenly Parents—as partners and unified team, working side by side in all matters relating to creation and their children.[22] There are "historical portrayals of Heavenly Mother as procreator and parent, as a divine person, as co-creator of worlds, as co-framer of the plan of salvation with the Father, and as a concerned and loving parent involved in our mortal probation."[23]

To date, apostles and prophets from The Church of Jesus Christ of Latter-day Saints have not received definitive revelations on the nature, roles, and character of our Mother in Heaven. Most of what the leaders have gleaned emanates from doctrinal concepts and the understanding of motherhood, the plan of salvation, and godhood. But it only seems logical that a Heavenly Mother watches over and is just as involved with her children as Heavenly Father. This knowledge can be a source of comfort and strength.

"Sometimes we think the whole job is up to us, forgetful that there are loved ones beyond our sight who are thinking about us and our children," wrote Harold B. Lee. "We forget that we have a Heavenly Father and a Heavenly Mother who are even more concerned, probably, than our earthly father and mother, and that influences from beyond are constantly working to try to help us when we do all we can."[24]

While there are not direct references in the scriptures to a Heavenly Mother, we do have allusions and clues. For instance, Charles Penrose, editor of the *Deseret News,* in as early as 1902 wrote an article that it was the feminine gender used in Genesis when the divine spirit moved upon the face of the waters.[25] And Alma 42:24 reads: "For behold, justice exerciseth all his demands, and also mercy claimeth all which is her own; and thus, none but the truly penitent are saved." Notice the personal pronouns for justice and mercy.

WHY WE DON'T PRAY TO HEAVENLY MOTHER

Church leaders have used various reverential titles to refer to Heavenly Mother, such as "God the Mother," "Mother God", and "Eternal Mother."[26] Brigham Young taught calling our Heavenly Mother "God" is consistent with our doctrine and the Genesis account of Adam and Eve created in the image of God.[27] However, it must be clear that we pray only to Heavenly Father. When the divine appeared to Joseph Smith in the First Vision, Heavenly Father's will was that only He and Jesus, His son, were revealed at that time.

However, Rudger Clawson taught, "It doesn't take from our worship of the Eternal Father, to adore our Eternal Mother, any more than it diminishes the love we bear our earthly fathers, to include our earthly mothers in our affections. . . . We honor woman when we acknowledge Godhood in her eternal prototype."[28]

Some people, both inside and outside of the Church's faith, question the practice of praying only to a Heavenly Father and not to Heavenly Mother. President Gordon B. Hinckley researched, looking "for any instance where any President of the Church . . . has offered a prayer to 'our Mother in Heaven.'"[29] Finding none, he nonetheless reiterated that "the fact that we do not pray to our Mother in Heaven in no way belittles or denigrates her."[30] As there is very little revelation about our Mother in Heaven, no one can add to or reduce Her glory and magnitude. By logic, she must be equal in glory and honor as she sits beside—in Her own throne—Her spouse, our Heavenly Father.

The Church follows a pattern for prayer already prescribed by Jesus Christ:

> But thou, when thou prayest, enter into thy closet, and when thou hast shut thy door, *pray to thy Father* which is in secret; and

thy Father which seeth in secret shall reward thee openly.

But when ye pray, use not vain repetitions, as the heathen *do:* for they think that they shall be heard for their much speaking.

Be not ye therefore like unto them: for your *Father* knoweth what things ye have need of, before *ye ask him.*

After this manner therefore pray ye: *Our Father which art in heaven*, Hallowed be thy name.[31]

We do not pray to a Heavenly Mother because we follow the example of the Savior, who taught His disciples, and us, to whom and how to pray. Jesus Christ set the pattern, and we follow His example.[32]

We pray to a Heavenly Father through his son Jesus Christ. But as there is a Heavenly Mother ruling by His side, there can be little doubt that she is aware of Her children's prayers and desires.

VEILS

References about our Heavenly Mother are, at best, veiled in the holy scriptures.[33] But as we discuss the reasons behind our obscure understanding of a veiled Holy Mother, it might be helpful to discuss the symbolism and power of veils.

According to the Church website, *veil* is "a word used in the scriptures to mean (1) a divider separating areas of the tabernacle or temple, (2) a symbol for a separation between God and man, (3) a thin cloth worn by people to cover their face or head, or (4) a God-given forgetfulness that blocks people's memories of the premortal existence."[34] In reading the scriptures, we find that it was not uncommon for both men and women to veil their faces, especially for a specific ceremony or practice.[35] Several excellent examples in the Bible give understanding of why something or someone would be veiled. In both Exodus and Leviticus, we read of the Holy of Holies as being veiled and separated from the rest of the tabernacle. God instructs Moses that Aaron is only to enter on specific occasions "that he die not."

Death? Special permission? Without proper authority or a proper sacrifice, anyone entering the Holy of Holies would die. This suggests a great, sacred power involved. The veil is erected to protect not what is *inside*, but to protect what is on the *outside*.

Another example is from Moses himself. He wore a veil after coming down from the mount, after having just spoken with God. We read that "the children of Israel saw the face of Moses, that the skin of Moses' face shone: and Moses put the veil upon his face again."[36] Moses did not need the veil when speaking with God, only with the frightened children of Israel who were not yet ready for this additional light, power, and knowledge that Moses possessed.

The scriptures also refer to God and the earth being covered with a veil. When that veil is removed, we shall see God as He is. We are to prepare ourselves now to be ready and worthy to see Him without being consumed along with the corruptible things, so we are ready for that "knowledge and glory [that will] dwell upon all the earth."[37]

A veil is also a forgetting, lovingly placed by our Heavenly Father. If we have not been given very much information about a Heavenly Mother, it is not necessarily as church subculture has hypothesized in the past, that She—the Mother—needed protection. It is *us* that need protection. We are not yet ready for her power. But like the woman in the wilderness,[38] one day the veil shall be rent, or dropped, and She will re-emerge when we are ready. We see signs that the veil is thinning in regard to our Heavenly Mother. But the full reveal of her existence in our lives and in the scriptures may not take place in this mortal life.

For now, we speak of Her with less than ideal knowledge. But one day "we all, with open faces beholding as in a glass the glory of the Lord [and our Heavenly Mother], are changed into the same image from glory to glory, even as by the Spirit of the Lord."[39] And with that knowledge we will have liberty.[40]

ENDNOTES

1. See for instance Genesis 1:26–27; 2:17; 3:22; Psalm 82:6; John 10:33–34; Matthew 5:48; 2 Peter 1:4; Acts 17:29; Romans 8:16–17; Revelation 3:21

2. Genesis 2:17; 3:22
   "Latter-day Saints see all people as children of God in a full
   and complete sense; they consider every person divine in origin,
   nature, and potential. Each has an eternal core and is 'a beloved
   spirit son or daughter of heavenly parents.' Each possesses seeds of
   divinity and must choose whether to live in harmony or tension
   with that divinity" (Topics, ChurchofJesusChrist.org/topics/
   becoming-like-god?lang=eng).
3. Dallin H. Oaks, "Apostasy and Restoration," *Ensign,* May 1995,
   84. See also, Doctrine and Covenants 132:19–20.
4. Abraham 3:13
5. See also Linda P. Wilcox, "The Mormon Concept of a Mother in
   Heaven," *Sisters in Spirit*, ed. Maureen U. Beecher and Livina F.
   Anderson. (Urbana, IL, 1987).
6. Joseph Fielding Smith, in *Answers to Gospel Questions*, vol. 3 (Salt
   Lake City, UT: Deseret Book, 1993), 144.
7. ChurchofJesusChrist.org states, "We have been given sufficient
   knowledge to appreciate the sacredness of this *doctrine* and to
   comprehend the divine pattern established for us as children of
   heavenly parents" (emphasis added).
8. "My Father in Heaven," in "Poetry, for the Times and Seasons,"
   Times and Seasons 6 (Nov. 15, 1845): 1039; "O My Father,"
   Hymns, no. 292
9. Wilford Woodruff, *The Discourses of Wilford Woodruff*, 62, ed. G.
   Homer Durham (Salt Lake City, 1968).
10. "The Origin of Man," *Improvement Era* 13, no. 1 (Nov. 1909):
    78.
11. See "Mother in Heaven," ChurchofJesusChrist.org Topics, Chur-
    chofJesusChrist.org/topics/mother-in-heaven?lang=eng.
    There is actually an account (third hand) related by Zebedee Col-
    trin where he states that he, Joseph Smith, and Sidney Rigdon
    received a vision after praying in the woods. In the full account
    all three saw Heavenly Father sitting on a throne accompanied
    by Heavenly Mother and Jesus Christ (Abraham H. Cannon,
    Journal, 25 August 1980, LDS Church Archives).
12. See for instance *Journal of Discourses* 9:286, 11:122, 26:214.
    "If modern scripture is correct, a woman's godhood, which, like a
    man's, is 'above all' and encompasses 'all power,' is neither limited

nor subservient. No distinctions are made as to the dimensions of male and female godhood" (Carol Cornwall Madsen, "Mormon Women and the Temple: Toward a New Understanding," *Sisters in Spirit: Mormon Women in Historical and Cultural Perspective*, 99, edited by Maureen Ursenbach Beecher and Lavina Fielding Anderson).

13. James E. Talmage, speech in Tabernacle on 27 April 1902, *Deseret News*, April 28, 1902.

Early leaders such as George Q. Cannon, Orson F. Whitney, and B.H. Roberts taught the doctrine of a Heavenly Mother who stood side by side with our Father and that women were made in the image of Heavenly Father's wife and partner. For instance, see George Q. Cannon, "Mr. Canon's [*sic*] Lecture," *Salt Lake Daily Herald*, April 15, 1884, 8.

Orson F. Whitney, "Bishop O. F. Whitney," *Woman's Exponent 24* (June 15, 1895): 9.

14. Hebrews 12:9

15. Elaine Anderson Cannon, "Mother in Heaven," *The Encyclopedia of Mormonism*, May 27, 2011, eom.byu.edu/index.php/Mother_in_Heaven.

16. Sharon Eubank, "This is a Woman's Church", FAIR Conference, August 8, 2014, fairmormon.org/perspectives/fair-conferences/2014–fairmormon-conference/womans-church.

17. Susan Young Gates, "The Vision Beautiful," *Improvement Era*, 1919, vol. 23, 542.

18. Paul Massari, "Exclusion or God's Plan: Interview with David F. Holland," Harvard Divinity School, June 25, 2014, hds.harvard.edu/news/2014/06/25/exclusion-or-god%E2%80%99s-plan#.

19. Jeffrey R. Holland, "Behold Thy Mother." The Church of Jesus Christ of Latter-day Saints, October 2015, ChurchofJesusChrist.org/general-conference/2015/10/behold-thy-mother?lang=eng.

20. David L. Paulsen and Martin Pulido, "'A Mother There': A Survey of Historical Teachings about Mother in Heaven," *BYU Studies 50*, no. 1 (2011), 75.

21. Robert A. Rees, "Our Mother in Heaven," *Sunstone 15*, April 1991, 49–50.

22. For instance, see Boyd K. Packer, "Counsel to Young Men," *Ensign*, May 2009, 50; Thomas S. Monson, *An Invitation to*

Exaltation (Salt Lake City: Deseret Book, 1997) 2–4; Dallin H. Oaks, "Apostasy and Restoration," *Ensign,* May 1995, 84; M. Russell Ballard," Spiritual Development," October 1978 general conference; Brian K. Ashton, "The Father," October 2018 general conference; Neill F. Marriott, "What Shall We do?" April 2016 general conference.

23. Paulsen and Pulido, 76. The authors also note that they have compiled more than 600 discourses since 1844.

24. Harold B. Lee,"The Influence and Responsibility of Women," *Relief Society Magazine 51,* February 1964, 85.

25. Charles W. Penrose, "Women in Heaven," *Millennial Star* 64, June 26, 1902, 410.

26. Paulsen and Pulido, 90, footnote 33.

27. Genesis 1:26–27

28. Rudger Clawson, "Our Mother in Heaven," *Millennial Star 72* September 29, 1910, 619–20.
   For instance, Orson F. Whitney asked, "What is this but a virtual recognition of the feminine principle as well as the masculine principle of Deity?" ("Our Mother in Heaven His Theme," *Deseret Evening News,* July 16, 1906, 5).

29. Gordon B. Hinckley, "Daughters of God," The Church of Jesus Christ of Latter-day Saints, churchofjesuschrist.org/study/ensign/1991/11/daughters-of-god?lang=eng, accessed December 17, 2019.

30. Hinckley, ibid. Hinckley also reiterates that he believes those who advocate praying to a Heavenly Mother are well-meaning albeit misguided.

31. Matthew 6:6–9, emphasis added. See also 3 Nephi 18:19–21; John 17:1, 5, 21, 24–25; Matthew 4:10; Luke 4:8; 3 Nephi 13:9; 17:15.

32. For instance see Matthew 6:9, 3 Nephi 13:9, 17:15, 18:21, 19:19–21. Gordon B. Hinckley goes into more detail in his talk "Daughters of God," *Ensign,* November 1991.

33. Just as the name of Jesus is not found in the Old Testament (Jesus, of course, is the English translation of the Hebrew form of Yehoshua, Yeshua, and Yeshu, and the Greek rendering of Yeshua and Yeshu) it is not strange to see that reference to a Heavenly Mother is absent as well. "It is not clear why specific

information found on the brass plates—such as the use of the Savior's name in prophecy—was not included in the records now constituting the Old Testament. It is possible that the Lord's name originally appeared in the writings of the prophets, but was one of the 'plain and precious things taken away from the book.' (See 1 Ne. 13:28.) References to a heavenly mother may have been taken from the scriptures as well" (Stephen D. Ricks, "Did Old Testament prophets also know that the Lord's name would be Jesus Christ?" 1984, churchofjesuschrist.org/study/ensign/1984/09/i-have-a-question/did-old-testament-prophets-also-know-that-the-lords-name-would-be-jesus-christ?lang=eng).

34. ChurchofJesusChrist.org, "The Guide to the Scriptures," Veil, ChurchofJesusChrist.org/scriptures/gs/veil?lang=eng.

35. The practice of wearing veils continues to this day in differing cultures and religions. Unfortunately, often the true symbolism and meaning is corrupted and bastardized in a current mainstream culture that does not understand nor appreciate the beauty and poetry of such symbolism. Even today some cultures—including Islam—continue this practice, women covering their faces and heads when in the presence of non-family members or when engaging in religious practices.

36. Exodus 34: 35

37. Doctrine and Covenants 101:23–25

38. The JST of Revelation 8:5–7 refers to the woman as the church in the latter days. However, most scripture has dual or more meanings as most students and scholars of such books as Isaiah can attest.

39. 2 Corinthians 3:16–18

40. 2 Corinthians 3:17

Chapter 16

WHAT DOES IT MEAN TO PRESIDE?

In the home it [presiding] is a partnership
with husband and wife equally yoked
together, sharing in decisions,
always working together.

—Boyd K. Packer

PRESIDING AND THE PRIESTHOOD

In the 1995 "The Family: A Proclamation To The World," we read that "fathers and mothers are obligated to help one another as equal partners" and also that "by divine design, fathers are to preside over their families in love and righteousness and are responsible to provide the necessities of life and protection for their families."[1]

We are living in the time of restoration, an ongoing process, according to Elder Uchtdorf. "It includes 'all that God has revealed, all that He does now reveal,' and the 'many great and important things' that 'He will yet reveal'. . . . The exciting developments of today are part of that long-foretold period of preparation that will culminate in the glorious Second Coming of our Savior, Jesus Christ."[2] The ongoing restoration includes greater clarification on the role of women and their co-equal role in the family government as well as Church leadership.

Current revelation reveals that through the patriarchal order both husband and wife preside over a family. But, if mothers and fathers are equal, what does *preside* mean? It was President Spencer W. Kimball who first replaced the word *rule* with the softer *preside* with the explicit directive that wives are to exercise full partnership in marriages.[3] (This is another example of continuing revelation, unveiling more information about roles and relationships.) However, President Kimball and the General Authorities since then have not provided a definitive list of what presiding in the home entails.

What we do have is a clear distinction of what it is *not*:

That the rights of the priesthood are inseparably connected with the powers of heaven, and that the powers of heaven cannot be controlled nor handled only upon the principles of righteousness.

That they may be conferred upon us, it is true; but when we undertake to cover our sins, or to gratify our pride, our vain ambition, or to exercise control or dominion or compulsion upon the souls of the children of men, in any degree of unrighteousness, behold, the heavens withdraw themselves; the Spirit of the Lord is grieved; and when it is withdrawn, Amen to the priesthood or the authority of that man.

No power or influence can or ought to be maintained by virtue of the priesthood, only by persuasion, by long-suffering, by gentleness and meekness, and by love unfeigned;

By kindness, and pure knowledge, which shall greatly enlarge the soul without hypocrisy, and without guile—

Reproving betimes with sharpness, when moved upon by the Holy Ghost; and then showing forth afterwards an increase of love toward him whom thou hast reproved, lest he esteem thee to be his enemy;

That he may know that thy faithfulness is stronger than the cords of death.

Let thy bowels also be full of charity towards all men, and to the household of faith, and let virtue garnish thy thoughts unceasingly; then shall thy confidence wax strong in the presence of God; and the doctrine of the priesthood shall distill upon thy soul as the dews from heaven.

The Holy Ghost shall be thy constant companion, and thy scepter an unchanging scepter of righteousness and truth; and thy dominion shall be an everlasting dominion, and without compulsory means it shall flow unto thee forever and ever.[4]

These verses give an unmistakable distinction between *rule* and *preside*, especially as used within the context of the priesthood.

CHURCH VERSUS HOME

Boyd K. Packer clarified, "In the Church there is a distinct line of authority. We serve where called by those who preside over us. *In the home it is a partnership* with husband and wife equally yoked together, sharing in decisions, always working together."[5]

As Elder L. Tom Perry reminded, "There is not a president or a vice president in a family. The couple works together eternally for the good of the family. . . . They are on equal footing. They plan and organize the affairs of the family jointly and unanimously as they move forward."[6]

In the Church the presiding officer has the final say. In the home the final say is an equal and unified decision that has been discussed by both the husband and wife. James E. Talmage said, "They two should form the governing head of the family institution. . . . Each separately pertain duties and functions which the other is less qualified to discharge."[7]

Elder Oaks shared the experience of his single mother presiding in the home after his father died, even after Elder Oaks had been ordained a deacon. She directed the family and called on who would say the prayer: "When my father died, my mother presided over our family. She had no priesthood office, but as the surviving parent in her marriage she had become the governing officer in her family. At the same time, she was always totally respectful of the priesthood authority of our bishop and other Church leaders. She presided over her family, but they presided over the Church."[8]

One priesthood holder, R. Bryant Siddoway (husband of the author), defined *preside* as "exercising priesthood keys." There is a difference between the power *of* and the power *in* the priesthood. Women are not ordained; hence, they do not exercise power *in* the priesthood. However, a righteous woman exercises power *of* the priesthood.

TO SERVE AND PROTECT

The Latin origin of the word *preside* is *praesidēre*[9] (its first known use wasn't until 1608), which means "to stand guard." So, to "sit in front of" comes more from the context of protection so that all those who he or she is "standing guard" over can progress, grow, and fulfill the measure of their creations in an atmosphere of love and security.

One who presides[10] is someone who defends, guards, watches over, and protects. With this definition we can clearly see that both husbands and wives preside in the family, defending and protecting in respective roles. A righteous husband and father who truly wants to preside will provide an atmosphere that is safe enough to allow and give all members of the family a space to grow, progress, and reach their full God-given potential.[11]

Presiding has more to do with accountability rather than power, protection rather than domination,[12] and service rather than ruling.[13] A man who honors and magnifies his priesthood responsibilities will have one desire—that of the welfare of his entire family, providing the means and ways with love and gentle persuasion.[14]

Unfortunately, we still live in a world where some men ignore the potential offered with an equal presiding partnership. Abuse and neglect still occur, and some wives and children suffer regularly.

Richard G. Scott said, "In some cultures, tradition places a man in a role to dominate, control, and regulate all family affairs. That is not the way of the Lord. In some places the wife is almost owned by her husband, as if she were another of his personal possessions. That is a cruel, mistaken vision of marriage encouraged by Lucifer that every priesthood holder must reject. It is founded

WHAT DOES IT MEAN TO PRESIDE?

on the false premise that a man is somehow superior to a woman. Nothing could be farther from the truth."[15]

Through the Atonement and good examples of those men and women who preside over their families in righteousness, change can occur and hearts can be mended and knit together.

SOME THOUGHTS

The following are some general guidelines that both husbands and wives can follow to righteously preside in their home and over their families.

1. Know—and follow—the doctrines and principles of the restored gospel.
2. Work on improving oneself first. Elder Yasuo Niiyama wrote, "A husband and father [and wives and mothers] must first learn to love and govern himself before he can do so with others."[17] He and she must learn to govern wisely and never, ever abuse another living thing.
3. Acknowledge each other's roles and work together.
4. Exercise the priesthood righteously by learning how to love through the example of the Savior[16] and the influence of the Holy Ghost. Presiding as the Savior presides means giving one's life to his or her family.
5. Teach children the important things from the scriptures and his or her own righteous example.

Every mother is a matriarch just as every father is a patriarch. They are both accountable to God as they fulfill their often separate and distinct roles, all the while obligated to "help one another as equal partners."[18]

Hudson and Miller wrote, "Moreover, contrary to scripture and the teachings of latter-day prophets, some men and women have interpreted presiding to mean that after equal counsel, equal consent is not necessary because the presider (or husband) has the right of final say. In considering the equal partnership, both husband and wife have a sacred obligation to refrain from thoughts and actions that might undermine that equal partnership."[19]

Both husbands and wives are accountable to one another as they fulfill their respective roles. But if we were going to define presiding as it is symbolized in the temple and our understanding of the stewardship of the two trees, presiding in terms of stewardship is bringing the priesthood into the home.[20] Eve and her daughters guard the veil from heaven into mortality and family. Adam and his sons guard the ordinances of the priesthood, bringing it into the home as he presides in righteousness and obedience. Every home deserves to have a minister of Christ serving there.

ENDNOTES

1. ChurchofJesusChrist.org/topics/family-proclamation?lang=eng
2. Dieter F. Uchtdorf, "Are You Sleeping through the Restoration?" The Church of Jesus Christ of Latter-day Saints, April 2014, ChurchofJesusChrist.org/general-conference/2014/04/are-you-sleeping-through-the-restoration?lang=eng
3. Spencer W. Kimball and Edward L. Kimball, in *The Teachings of Spencer W. Kimball* (Salt Lake City, UT: Deseret Book, 1982), 315.
4. Doctrine and Covenants 121:36–37, 41–46
5. Boyd K. Packer, "The Relief Society," *Ensign,* May 1998, 73, emphasis added.
6. L. Tom Perry, "Fatherhood, an Eternal Calling," *Ensign,* May 2004, 71, emphasis added.
7. James E. Talmage, "The Eternity of Sex," *Young Woman's Journal,* October 1914.
8. Dallin H. Oaks, "Priesthood Authority in the Family and the Church," The Church of Jesus Christ of Latter-day Saints, ChurchofJesusChrist.org/general-conference/2005/10/priesthood-authority-in-the-family-and-the-church?lang=eng, accessed December 10, 2019.
9. dictionary.com/browse/preside; merriam-webster.com/dictionary/preside
10. "In the perspective of the gospel, 'leadership' does not mean the right to dictate, command, and order. On the contrary, it means to guide, protect, point the way, set the example, make secure, inspire, and create a desire to sustain and follow. Literally, the

husband is to lead the way" (*The Savior, the Priesthood and You* [Melchizedek Priesthood course of study, 1973–74], 172).

11. President Howard W. Hunter wrote, "A righteous father protects his children with his time and the presence in their social, educational, and spiritual activities and responsibilities" ("Being a Righteous Husband and Father," *Ensign*, Nov. 1994, 51). See also Doctrine and Covenants 75:28.

12. Doctrine and Covenants 121:39

13. "Whosoever will be great among you, let him be your minister; and whosoever will be chief among you, let him be your servant" (Matthew 20:25–27).

14. Doctrine and Covenants 121

15. Richard G. Scott, "Honor the Priesthood and Use It Well," *Ensign*, November 2008, 46. Gordon B. Hinckley also said, "A warning accompanies this sacred duty of presiding, especially when one holds the priesthood. No man is worthy of the priesthood who abuses his wife, the mother of his children. . . . You cannot enter the highest degree of glory in the kingdom of heaven unless you go there walking hand in hand with your companion at your side" (Fireside at Copenhagen, Denmark, June 14, 1996, *Ensign*, August 1997, 4). ChurchofJesusChrist.org/ensign/1997/08/inspirational-thoughts?lang=eng

16. Doctrine and Covenants 121:41–43

17. These guidelines are adapted from an article written by Elder Yasuo Niiyama, former Area Authority Seventy Asia North Area.ChurchofJesusChrist.org/ensign/2004/02/presiding-righteously-in-the-home?lang=eng. Yasuo Niiyama, "Presiding Righteously in the Home," *Ensign*, February 2004.

18. ChurchofJesusChrist.org/topics/family-proclamation?lang=eng

19. Valerie M. Hudson and Richard B. Miller, "Equal Partnership in Marriage," The Church of Jesus Christ of Latter-day Saints, ChurchofJesusChrist.org/ensign/2013/04/equal-partnership-in-marriage?lang=eng, accessed December 10, 2019.

20. See also Dallin H. Oaks, "The Powers of the Priesthood," The Church of Jesus Christ of Latter-day Saints, ChurchofJesusChrist.org/general-conference/2018/04/the-powers-of-the-priesthood?lang=eng

Chapter 17
THE HARD QUESTIONS

*Hold fast to what you already know
and stand strong until additional
knowledge comes.*

—Elder Jeffrey R. Holland

Any questions we seek the answers to must be "approached with unity and respect."[1] This is the way to invite the Holy Ghost, the member of the Godhead that carries the truth of all things to our hearts.

ARE WOMEN REALLY TO SUBMIT TO THEIR HUSBANDS?

One of the harder subjects to understand and explain is Ephesians 5:21–24: "Wives, submit yourselves unto your own husbands, as unto the Lord. For the husband is the head of the wife, even as Christ is the head of the church: and he is the saviour of the body. Therefore as the church is subject unto Christ, so let the wives be to their own husbands in every thing."

Paul is a classic example of someone who intermingled the Christian *doctrine* with the Jewish *culture*. In the epistles attributed to Paul (some scholars question whether all of the letters were indeed authored by him),[2] much of what is written is taken out of context. It must be taken into account that Paul was giving advice and answering questions in the different units of the Church at that time. Different units received different doctrinal extrapolations based on need and circumstance. When Paul spoke about women, his sermons contained Christian doctrine with a heavy mixture of Jewish culture.[3]

Jolene Rockwood writes,[4] "For example, he tells the Corinthians that he approves of women praying and prophesying in the church (Christian principle), as long as they cover their heads (Jewish tradition)."[5] The culture of that day demanded that women cover their heads as a sign of shame.[6] Paul is working from the inside out of the culture of that branch of the church.

Let's also take this scripture (Ephesians 5: 21–24) in conjunction with Doctrine and Covenants 25:5. Women are to comfort their husbands. In Ephesians, Paul is comparing wives to Christ (as later he does the same with husbands). So wives—and husbands—are to submit as Christ submits, standing by their husband's side as Christ stands by our side, comforting and having an "obligation to maintain loving affection and to provide consideration and thoughtfulness."[7]

Just like Jesus, Paul was giving counsel and teaching concepts using *his* day, for his *culture*. Horton reminds us that "revelation and certain scriptural injunctions are adapted to the circumstances of a given time."[8] Gospel restoration has been line upon line down throughout the ages, feeding milk to those who are not ready for meat, and allowing meat for those spiritually mature and ready for more.

Another problem arises when we use this scripture out of context. The passages before and after suggest a submission of *both* partners for the good of the family and the marriage as well as the entire body of the Church.

PLURAL MARRIAGE

When apostles and prophets of *any* dispensation have given counsel, it is wise for us to take into account the culture and context of that time. For instance, Jacob in the Book of Mormon railed on the men of his time for taking on more than one wife. As any student of the scripture recognizes, there has been a time and a place for polygamy, and it is always predicated on a commandment from the Lord.[9] He decides when, where, who, and why.

During the early part of the nineteenth century, plural marriage was introduced, and it was instituted in the 1840s.[10] The practice was formally discontinued in 1890, by revelation through Wilford Woodruff. According to Gordon B. Hinckley, polygamy was practiced[11] by 2–5 percent of the members.[12] While many theories are suggested as to why the Lord would command this, including allowing widows and older women a chance for home, family, and security, the only *scriptural* justification is to raise up seed unto God.[13]

The divorce laws in the Utah Territory were surprisingly liberal, granting women divorce more easily than in the rest of the United States at that time. "As a rule," stated one of Brigham Young's clerks, "[President Young] rarely refuses a bill [of divorcement] on the application of a wife, and NEVER when she INSISTS on it."[14]

Once again, readers must be cautioned to observe historical events with the appropriate lens. Keep in mind an eternal perspective, and avoid imposing a current twenty-first-century lens with its accompanying norms, attitudes, and 20/20 hindsight.

In our culture, just the idea of plural marriage is a hard pill to swallow. And when it relates to the patriarchal order, it's one aspect of God's culture we can't wrap our minds around. There are no doctrinal scriptures that address this topic, but one can assume that parents preside over their own children and family.

As we have little doctrinal direction concerning the patriarchal order or its administration as it applies to plural marriages—both in this life and/or the next—it would be advantageous to mention just a couple of things concerning the practice in general.

It must be reiterated that what follows is merely the author's theological thoughts and not doctrinal opinions. What the Lord commands, the Lord commands.

In both biblical times and the early days of the Church, the Lord commanded some of His people to practice plural marriage. In Jacob 2:3, 27 we are instructed "that monogamy is the general law of marriage and polygamy is an *exception* to the general law, which exception *must be commanded by the Lord before it can be practiced.*"[15]

And what is the purpose of marriage? According to Valerie Hudson, the two-fold purpose is "to raise up righteous seed unto God" and "to prepare the marriage partners for eternal increase in the hereafter (D&C 132:19)."[16]

But an interesting note is the way D&C 132 is worded. Verses 32–33 state the mandate that temple marriage is a requisite for exaltation. But then in verse 34 the Lord says, "God commanded Abraham, and Sarah gave Hagar to Abraham to wife. And why did she do it?" (Another point of evidence of the partnership of the patriarchal order is that God commanded both of them, not just Abraham.)

It is interesting that God follows this discussion of polygamy— and ties it in with—the *law of sacrifice* (specifically God commanding Abraham to sacrifice his son despite the general law of thou shalt not kill). (See D&C 132:36.)

So, the Abrahamic sacrifice—the heaviest and most excruciating sacrifice—relates to the story of Hagar as much as it does to Isaac. God recognizes that polygamy, only to be entered in by commandment, is nonetheless an ultimate test of sacrifice and faith. Polygamy is not the general law; it is the *exception* to the law. Happiness about the sacrifice does not seem to be a requirement, just obedience. As we see what happened with Abraham *and* Isaac, a ram was provided in the thicket after Abraham and Isaac proved to themselves and to God that they would obey in all things, even by obedience to a lawful exception of a general law.

In terms of the patriarchal order, as we use Adam and Eve as a template, a woman is an equal partner as matriarch of her family, just as Hagar was matriarch over Ishmael.[17]

UNRIGHTEOUS DOMINION OVER WOMEN

If God honors and respects womanhood so much, why does He allow so much unrighteous dominion, inequality, and suffering at the hands of those who are supposed to protect? This question is the reason a discussion about the true nature of the patriarchal order is so necessary for both genders. It specifically discourages and makes it difficult for one spouse to exercise unrighteous dominion over the other. If both righteously preside over the family—in the sense of leadership, example, and protection—both are protected as they live within the bounds of that covenant and all the laws of Heavenly Father and Heavenly Mother.

Whatever anguish, trial, or sacrifice we are called to bear, endure it well, for it will eventually come to an end.

In the Doctrine and Covenants we learn, "It is the nature and disposition of almost all men, as soon as they get a little authority, as they suppose, [to] immediately exercise unrighteous dominion."[18]

A poignant example of this principle is in the Book of Mormon, when Alma and Amulek witnessed the mass murder of innocent women and children. Their torturers threw them into a raging fire built specifically for this purpose. When Amulek, struck with the pain of the scene, wanted to stretch forth his hand to stop the massacre, Alma stopped him, stating: "The Spirit constraineth me that I must not stretch forth mine hand; for behold the Lord receiveth them up unto himself, in glory; and he doth suffer that they may do this thing, or that the people may do this thing unto them, according to the hardness of their hearts, that the judgments which he shall exercise upon them in his wrath may be just; and the blood of the innocent shall stand as a witness against them, yea, and cry mightily against them at the last day."[19]

There have been, and will be, times when our happiness may be derailed for a time because of the choices of others. But when the weaknesses, frailties, and challenges of earth life are finally released along with the mortal body, women will be recompensed in full for all of the injustices heaped upon them: the abuse, the prejudice, the history of neglect that has been prevalent in the lives of so many sisters. God counts each tear shed by women, and will wipe them dry. Everything unfair will be made fair.

Elder Dale G. Renlund said, "[Mortals] say of some temporal suffering, 'No future bliss can make up for it,' not knowing that Heaven, once attained, will work backwards and turn even that agony into a glory. . . . The Blessed will say, 'We have never lived anywhere except in Heaven.'"[20]

It must be remembered that Heavenly Father even allowed His most perfect Son, Jesus Christ, to suffer the most excruciating pain, all with a divine purpose. Are we less loved?

Joseph B. Wirthlin promised, "The Lord compensates the faithful for every loss. That which is taken away from those who love the Lord will be added unto them in His own way. While it may not come at the time we desire, the faithful will know that every tear today will eventually be returned a hundredfold with tears of rejoicing and gratitude."[21]

THE UNBELIEVING SPOUSE

In a church that emphasizes eternal families and a culture that stresses "no empty chairs,"[22] confusion and heartache can arise in a less than ideal family unit. Satan stirs within those aching hearts the fear of an eternity of aloneness. What of the patriarchal order, of eternal marriage, when the threads begin to unravel in the "Families Are Forever" cross-stitch sampler? This is a difficult one, especially if a couple originally entered into matrimony on the same page and sharing the same goals, and then somewhere down the line one spouse decides that he or she no longer believes in the same destiny.

The decision to sever any or all ties with a disbelieving spouse should be done with prayer, fasting, and with the counsel of an inspired church leader. The pain associated with living with a partner who once held the same views, positions, and beliefs in the same principles cannot be understated. Platitudes often serve the messenger more than the receiver.

Obviously, such a decision is not to be taken lightly, nor is counsel or advice given on the subject. With that in mind, the following are some thoughts on this challenging situation.

The Apostle Paul recognized the power of a righteous example of the faithful spouse, coupled with love. He counseled,

> If any brother hath a wife that believeth not, and she be pleased to dwell with him, let him not put her away. And the woman which hath an husband that believeth not, and if he be pleased to dwell with her, let her not leave him. For the unbelieving husband is sanctified by the wife, and the unbelieving wife is sanctified by the husband: else were your children unclean; but now are they holy. . . . For what knowest thou, O wife, whether thou shalt save thy husband? or how knowest thou, O man, whether thou shalt save thy wife?[23]

God will sanctify our difficult days, and with our obedience can sanctify our spouse. What power!

We have been promised that because of and through the Atonement, everything that was unfair in this life will eventually be made fair. At times it is hard to imagine how all can possibly be well. But the grace of God covers everything.

So how does the patriarchal order work in a situation such as this? A faithful member can still enter into and keep covenants made in the holy temple. Even if the marriage is dissolved, the covenants made in the temple are also with God and cannot be dissolved except through unfaithfulness to those covenants. For instance, any children born in the covenant (to parents after they were sealed in the temple) are still sealed to these parents, even if the "parents' temple sealing to each other is canceled."[24] individual's termination of temple covenants through unfaithfulness or divorce does not cancel out the faithful spouse's covenants.

SOME REMAINING THOUGHTS ON SOME OF LIFE'S HARD QUESTIONS

The ChurchofJesusChrist.org's section "Becoming like God" contains comforting reflection:

> Latter-day Saints tend to imagine exaltation through the lens of the sacred in mortal experience. They see the seeds of godhood in the joy of bearing and nurturing children and the intense love they

feel for those children, in the impulse to reach out in compassionate service to others, in the moments they are caught off guard by the beauty and order of the universe, in the grounding feeling of making and keeping divine covenants.

Church members imagine exaltation less through images of what they will *get* and more through the relationships they have now and how those relationships might be purified and elevated. As the scriptures teach, "That same sociality which exists among us here will exist among us there, only it will be coupled with eternal glory, which glory we do not now enjoy."[25]

And then comes this glorious promise: "Christ's Atonement not only provides forgiveness from sin and victory over death, it also *redeems imperfect relationships*, heals the spiritual wounds that stifle growth, and strengthens and enables individuals to develop the attributes of Christ."[26]

God does not require yoking two unequal beings together for eternity. A spouse that finds him or herself in such a position is to stay on the covenant path. For now, you are preparing yourself to function, at a future date, as a full partner with an equally faithful mate.[27] No blessing will be withheld from the obedient.

ENDNOTES

1. Sharon Eubank, "Being a Woman: An Eternal Perspective," The Church of Jesus Christ of Latter-day Saints, August 2016, churchofjesuschrist.org/study/ensign/2016/08/being-a-woman-an-eternal-perspective?lang=eng.

2. For instance, New Testament scholar George Arthur Buttrick believes that the passage in 1 Timothy 2:9–15 was written by someone other than Paul but that it was attributed to the Apostle (*The Interpreter's Dictionary of the Bible*, 3:683 and 4:651).

3. For instance, L.R. Iannaccone (in "Let the Women Be Silent," *Sunstone* 7 [May–June 1982]: 39–45) suggests that in 1 Corinthians 14:34–35 Paul is actually quoting a line in the letter he received from Corinth (and which he answers with incredulity in verse 36).

4. Jolene Edmunds Rockwood, "The Redemption of Eve," in *Sisters in Spirit: Mormon Women in Historical and Cultural Perspective*,

ed. Maureen Ursenbach. Beecher and Lavina Fielding Anderson (Urbana, I: University of Illinois Press, 1992), 15.

5. 1 Corinthians 11:5

6. Louis Ginzberg, in *The Legends of the Jews*, vol. 1 (Baltimore, MD: Johns Hopkins University Press, 1998), 67.

7. Spencer W. Kimball, "Fundamental Principles to Ponder and Live," The Church of Jesus Christ of Latter-day Saints, churchofjesuschrist.org/study/general-conference/1978/10/fundamental-principles-to-ponder-and-live?lang=eng, accessed December 17, 2019.

8. George A. Horton, "How Can We Tell Which Scriptures Can Be Likened to All of Us and Which Ones Cannot?," Church of Jesus Christ, accessed December 17, 2019, churchofjesuschrist.org/study/ensign/1994/01/i-have-a-question/how-can-we-tell-which-scriptures-can-be-likened-to-all-of-us-and-which-ones-cannot.html?lang=eng

9. For example, David and Solomon are condemned for having multiple wives, where Abraham and Jacob of the Old Testament are not. The difference is that the latter were commanded, whereas the former took additional wives that were not sanctioned by the Lord. (See Doctrine and Covenants 132:34–39 and Jacob 2:27, 30).

10. See Doctrine and Covenants 132.

11. "Nineteenth-century Mormon women, in both plural and monogamous marriages, were not just interested in raising families and blindly following their husbands. They were politically active and participated in territorial elections. Many were well connected with national women's organizations. These women also taught school and were active in publishing and literary activities. Some even served their communities by going to medical school and becoming skilled physicians. Because of their competence and level of self-reliance, they did not have to resort to public assistance.

    "Unlike the contemporary practice . . . in [today's polygamous groups] 19th century plural marriage among members of The Church of Jesus Christ of Latter-day Saints was not controlled by the arbitrary authority of one individual. On the contrary, decisions related to marriage were settled by consideration of the feelings of all interested parties. Furthermore, the consent of individual women was always honored in any marriage proposal. Though there was some social and cultural pressure, it was not determinative. Both men and women were free to refuse offers of marriage they found unacceptable.

"Brigham Young did not arrange marriages unless he was asked to, and he readily granted divorces. Far from the misconceptions of life-long servitude to the absolute power of the patriarchy, this non-legalistic system of divorce allowed women considerable autonomy" (Marlin K. Jensen, May 5, 2008, Mormonnewsroom.org, mormonnewsroom.org/commentary/polygamy-then-and-now).

12. This number varies by different historians, some claiming 20–30 percent average.
13. Jacob 2:27–30
14. Jessie L. Embry, in *Mormon Polygamous Families: Life in the Principle* (Salt Lake City, UT: University of Utah Press, 1987), 253.
15. A. Don Sorensen and Valerie M. Hudson, "Chapter 7—Polygamy." Essay in *Women in Eternity, Women of Zion* (Springville, UT: CFI, 2004), 188, emphasis added
16. Ibid.
17. There is an excellent discussion by Valerie Hudson about polygamy as it is presented in D&C 132 and Jacob. See A. Don Sorensen and Valerie M. Hudson, "Chapter 7—Polygamy." Essay in *Women in Eternity, Women of Zion* (Springville, UT: CFI, 2004).
18. Doctrine and Covenants 121:39
19. Alma 14:10–11
20. Dale G. Renlund quoting C.S. Lewis in "Family History and Temple Work: Sealing and Healing," ChurchofJesusChrist.org/general-conference/2018/04/family-history-and-temple-work-sealing-and-healing?lang=eng
21. Joseph B. Wirthlin, "Come What May, and Love It," *Ensign*, November 2008, 28.
22. This is a phrase that originated with President Ezra Taft Benson in the late 1980s. As a young father, and then later as a church leader, Benson emphasized that there should be "no empty chairs" in the eternities)(Sheri L. Dew, *Ezra Taft Benson: A Biography* (1987), 363; *The Teachings of Ezra Taft Benson* (1988), 493).

23. 1 Corinthians 7:12–16
24. "If My Parents Were Sealed in the Temple and Then Got Divorced, Which One Am I Sealed to?," The Church of Jesus Christ of Latter-day Saints, August 2015, churchofjesuschrist. org/study/new-era/2015/08/to-the-point/if-my-parents-were-sealed-in-the-temple-and-then-got-divorced-which-one-am-i-sealed-to?lang=eng
25. Topics, ChurchofJesusChrist.org, ChurchofJesusChrist.org/topics/becoming-like-god?lang=eng. See also Doctrine and Covenants 130:2.
26. Ibid. See also Alma 7:11–12, emphasis added.
27. Ida Smith, "The Lord As a Role Model for Men and Women," *Ensign*, August 1980, 66–67.

Chapter 18

SINGLE WOMEN AND THE PATRIARCHAL ORDER

*Your purpose is not to fill a role, but
to build [His] kingdom.*

—Karen Anderson

It is no simple task to be a single woman in a culturally family-centric church. Those who are married appear to singles to have succeeded with some magic formula, and sometimes seem only to offer trite phrases that do little to comfort a faithful single sister.

This is not to belittle the "you'll be blessed in the eternities" talk. But for anyone going through a difficult time, validation is also needed now, not just in the eternities. Satan takes great delight in whispering lies into the ears of the single members, suggesting that leaving the Church would be so much easier, that "eternity" will never arrive.

It's unfair, at least by mortal standards, that many single members, especially sisters, are unmarried through no fault of their own. Their single status is not an indication that they are lazy or that there is some inherent flaw in them.

Even Elder Dallin H. Oaks acknowledges that "the princi-ples . . . identified for the exercise of priesthood authority are more understandable and more comfortable for a married woman than for a single woman, especially a single woman who has never been married. She does not now experience priesthood authority in the partnership relationship of marriage. Her experiences with priesthood authority are in the hierarchical relationships of the Church, and some single women feel they have no voice in those relationships."[1]

We admire faithful single members for keeping at it day after day, and week after week. The *Ensign* family" is a hard ideal to live up to. Singles are not fools for keeping at it, for not giving up. Cov-enant-keeping singles are amazing for continuing to hope and serve and love. Being single in The Church of Jesus Christ of Latter-day Saints is *not* for the faint of heart.

Most church members desire to have a companion and to have children. As Al Haines, former Klein Texas Stake President and cur-rent sealer at the Houston Texas Temple articulated, "The covenant path is highly customized, of when we enter it and when we com-plete it. . . . [As a church culture] we have allowed ourselves to be sort of wrapped up around this sequential axle of 'grow up, mission, marriage, school, etc.' We think life will then be complete, but that's actually the problem. We don't talk about life except in the context of you do A, B, C, and then you live happily ever after. What if it doesn't happen like that? Then we think we're a failure."

But the fact is, eternal life is not a point in time. It becomes very difficult for us to comprehend and understand eternal life (in this life) because of two very important reasons: constraints of time and space.

Neal A. Maxwell wrote, "Time is clearly not our natural dimen-sion. Thus it is that we are never really at home in time. Alternately, we find ourselves wishing to hasten the passage of time or to hold back the dawn. We can do neither, of course, but whereas the fish is at home in water, we are clearly not at home in time—because we belong to eternity."[2]

Alma tried explaining this to his son Corianton when he taught, "All is as one day with God, and time only is measured unto men."[3]

But know this: no matter your marital status, family status, gender, or nationality, your journey is every bit as significant as anyone else's. All of us, regardless of any of the above-mentioned differences, must get on and *stay on* the covenant path. An endowed single sister is allowed to do everything in the temple that a married sister is allowed. The endowment is the key.

WHAT IS YOUR PURPOSE?

There are two cultural camps[4] in the Church: *epicureanism*, which emphasizes celebrating life now, and *asceticism*, which emphasizes self-denial. Members of the second camp might say, "Just wait, and you'll find happiness in the next life." Members who may not be going through the same type of trial—where "trial" may be defined as suffering the delay of a specific blessing—inadvertently tend to offer such advice. Single sisters are currently delayed with regard to marriage and often children.

Elder Neal A. Maxwell wrote, "Some undergo searing developments that cut suddenly into mortality's status quo. Some have trials to pass through, while still others have allotments they are to live with."[5]

The purpose of faithful sisters on the covenant path is to build the kingdom of God. President Russell M. Nelson wisely said, "No one can do what a righteous woman can do. . . . My dear sisters, we need *you*! We need *your* strength, *your* conversion, *your* conviction, *your* ability to lead, *your* wisdom, and *your* voices. We simply cannot gather Israel without you."[6]

The gathering of Israel is "the greatest challenge, the greatest cause, and the greatest work on earth today."[7] So when we think of our work in this life, our personal missions and ministries, we are to search for and understand our spiritual gifts.

Even though we may never know "the meaning of all things"[8] in this life, especially in the context of delayed blessings, our goal is to be aligned with God's will for us. With this acceptance will come a self-assuredness, and "then shall [thy] confidence wax strong."[9] Maxwell referred to this as poise and quiet acceptance.[10] He promised that

that acceptance and quiet, self-assured confidence "is its own form of being 'anxiously engaged'[11] but without all the bells and whistles."[12] We can certainly be anxiously engaged without being anxious.

Writer Karen Anderson, after being diagnosed with infertility, went through her own soul-searching to find her purpose and mission in life. This is how she articulated her findings:

> The highest and holiest calling in this life is discipleship; you are called to be a disciple with your parents, children, friends, acquaintances, coworkers, strangers. Whatever path in life God gives you is the most important thing He has for you to do [right now]. If you are not married, are childless, or LGBT, etc., it is because what God has given you is more important for you than the other. Finding and filling your mission in life is the noblest thing you can do.
>
> [It is disheartening] that the message I receive as infertile is that I don't get to experience the purpose of life here—so my job is to endure and wait it out. I reject that message wholeheartedly. It's damaging to tell someone their mortal life is a placeholder.

Anderson continues: "When my answer to prayer was 'your purpose is not to fill a role but build my kingdom,' my life gratefully re-centered on Christ, as it should have been from the start. I had to reject other messages I was hearing to find my place in the first group."

Don't get caught up in the culture. Focus on Jesus Christ and His doctrine.

MOTHER OF ROME

It is an interesting side-note that the Roman goddess Vesta was a virgin goddess in charge of family relationships. Her symbol was the fire on the hearth, symbolizing her life, and her role was the guardian of life. She had no family of her own, and yet she was considered the mother of Rome, connecting all family relationships, creating communities, and, according to the ancient Romans, all of civilization. So married or not, with or without children, women weave things together. Women are the glue of relationships, the bridging of lives.

Women—mothers, wives, sisters, *all* females—regardless of how they define who they are in relation to those around them, have a divine privilege, ability, and gift to "heal and bind and create a generation of order."[13]

A DIVINE CALLING TO WAIT

A woman's role in the patriarchal order requires entering into the new and everlasting covenant of marriage in the temple by an authorized servant. And a righteous single woman, keeping her covenants, can be endowed, and exercise her God-given power.

As we are all living in a fallen world, walking through mists of darkness, not everyone is blessed with what he or she considers the ideal family. Many trials in this life involve the delay of something that is so desperately desired. Despite righteous desires and efforts, some women—and men—will not have the opportunity to marry in this life. Others will experience the heartaches of faulty or broken relationships.

Gordon B. Hinckley said, "Some who are not married . . . ask whether they will always be denied the highest degree of glory in that kingdom. I am confident that under the plan of a loving Father and a divine Redeemer, no blessing of which you are otherwise worthy will forever be denied you."[14] In the grand scheme and scale of the eternities that stretch behind and before us, these sufferings and loss of blessings will be but a small moment.[15]

Sometimes it's hard not to let past personal experiences cast "shadows over [our] hope,"[16] but God is aware, and He is watching over us. Elder Richard G. Scott promised:

> The Lord is intent on your personal growth and development. That progress is accelerated when you willingly allow Him to lead you through every growth experience you encounter, whether initially it be to your individual liking or not. When you trust in the Lord, when you are willing to let your heart and your mind be centered in His will, when you ask to be led by the Spirit to do His will, you are assured of the greatest happiness along the way and the most fulfilling attainment from this mortal experience. If you question everything you are asked to do, or dig in your heels at every unpleasant challenge, you make it harder for the Lord to bless you.[17]

SINGLE MOTHERS—YOU
ARE NOT FORGOTTEN

For those sisters who, for various reasons, are left to raise children on their own, the Lord has promised compensatory blessings.[18] When that partnership that is the ideal in a family is temporarily unavailable, the priesthood blessings are provided by those ministering brothers in the gospel of Jesus Christ. Blessings of health, sickness, and comfort can be administered by those faithful Melchizedek Priesthood holders.

The widow of Zarephath (current-day Lebanon) is a good example of a woman who was not forgotten by the Lord. It was this woman who Elijah was directed to minister to and to be ministered by. God knew her heart as well as He knew the condition and state that she and her son were in—suffering starvation in the middle of a famine with only enough meal and oil for one last meal. It took courage, faith, and trust in the Lord's servant to give Elijah the last of her food to eat. But she did so, her obedience blessing her and her son with enough food until the famine had ended.[19]

Isn't it interesting that out of all the suffering families in the land, the Lord sent Elijah to a *single mother*? He chose and trusted her to serve His servant. The Lord looks on every heart, and recognized her soul for what it was.

EVERY RIGHTEOUS DESIRE

As the faithful Latter-day Saint waits and obeys, Christ has left a promise to all those who seek justice and happiness. Elder Jeffrey Holland, in a BYU—Idaho devotional on seeking and achieving happiness, shared the following:

> Jesus gave the answer that rings from eternity to all eternity, "I am the way, the truth, and the life . . . And whatsoever ye shall ask in my name, that will I do . . . If ye shall ask any thing in my name, I will do it" . . . [20] What a promise! Live my way, live my truth, live my life—live in this manner that I am showing you and teaching you--and whatsoever you ask will be given, whatsoever you seek you will find, including happiness. Parts of the blessing may come soon, parts may come

later, and parts may not come until heaven but they will come—all of them . . . someday, sometime, somewhere you will have every righteous desire of your heart as you live the gospel of Jesus Christ.[21]

As Haines articulated, "I feel like the Lord has in store an incredible blessing for anybody who is being delayed, for whatever reason."

ENDNOTES

1. Dallin H. Oaks, "Priesthood Authority in the Family and the Church." The Church of Jesus Christ of Latter-day Saints, 2005, ChurchofJesusChrist.org/general-conference/2005/10/priesthood-authority-in-the-family-and-the-church?lang=eng

2. Neal A. Maxwell, "Patience," The Church of Jesus Christ of Latter-day Saints. An address delivered to students of Brigham Young University, November 27, 1979. ChurchofJesusChrist.org/study/ensign/1980/10/patience?lang=eng, accessed December 1, 2019;

3. Alma 40:8

4. There is an excellent 2015 blog post at *Wheat and Tares* entitled "The Great Chasm: Singles and Married," wheatandtares.org/2015/08/13/the-great-chasm-singles-and-married/?fbclid=IwAR1lBuQxXskNoS8OM0AkNxBo-xd4qZdKW80bxx9hD-IWM5–Aj8kscl4UuReI#comment-141483

5. Neal A. Maxwell, "Content with the Things Allotted unto Us," The Church of Jesus Christ of Latter-day Saints, April 2000, ChurchofJesusChrist.org/general-conference/2000/04/content-with-the-things-allotted-unto-us?lang=eng

6. Russell M. Nelson, "Sisters' Participation in the Gathering of Israel," The Church of Jesus Christ of Latter-day Saints, 2018, ChurchofJesusChrist.org/general-conference/2018/10/sisters-participation-in-the-gathering-of-israel?lang=eng

7. Russell M. Nelson and Wendy W. Nelson, "Hope of Israel," The Church of Jesus Christ of Latter-day Saints, 2018, ChurchofJesusChrist.org/study/broadcasts/worldwide-devotional-for-young-adults/2018/06/hope-of-israel?lang=eng

8. 1 Nephi 11:17

9. Doctrine and Covenants 121:45–46

10. Neal A. Maxwell, "Content with the Things Allotted unto Us,"

The Church of Jesus Christ of Latter-day Saints, April 2000, ChurchofJesusChrist.org/general-conference/2000/04/content-with-the-things-allotted-unto-us?lang=eng.

11. Doctrine and Covenants 58:27. See also Doctrine and Covenants 58:28.

12. Maxwell, ibid.

13. Sharon Eubank, "'This Is a Woman's Church,'" FairMormon, August 2014, airmormon.org/perspectives/fair-conferences/2014–fairmormon-conference/womans-church

14. Gordon B. Hinckley, "Daughters of God," *Ensign*, Nov. 1991, 98; ChurchofJesusChrist.org/study/ensign/1991/11/daughters-of-god?lang=eng

15. Doctrine and Covenants 121:7. See also Spencer W. Kimball, "The Righteous Role of Women," October 1979, ChurchofJesusChrist.org/general-conference/1979/10/the-role-of-righteous-women?lang=eng

16. Henry B. Eyring, "The Hope of Eternal Family Love," The Church of Jesus Christ of Latter-day Saints, August 2016, churchofjesuschrist.org/study/ensign/2016/08/the-hope-of-eternal-family-love?lang=eng

17. Richard G. Scott, "Finding Joy in Life," The Church of Jesus Christ of Latter-day Saints, ChurchofJesusChrist.org/general-conference/1996/04/finding-joy-in-life?lang=eng, accessed December 18, 2019.

18. Joseph Wirthlin promised, "The Lord compensates the faithful for every loss. That which is taken away from those who love the Lord will be added unto them in His own way. While it may not come at the time we desire, the faithful will know that every tear today will eventually be returned a hundredfold with tears of rejoicing and gratitude" ("Come What May, and Love It," *Ensign*, November 2008, 28; ChurchofJesusChrist.org/general-conference/2008/10/come-what-may-and-love-it?lang=eng).

19. 1 Kings 17: 9– 24, Luke 4:25–26

20. John 14:5–6, 13–14

21. Jeffrey R. Holland, "Living After the Manner of Happiness," Brigham Young University—Idaho, September 2014, byui.edu/devotionals/elder-jeffrey-r-holland.

Chapter 19

THE POWER AND PROMISE OF THE ATONEMENT

Beauty for ashes

oil of joy for mourning

the garment of praise

for the spirit of heaviness

that [we] might be called

trees of righteousness.

—Isaiah 61:3

Atonement means being as one or making whole. One of the themes of the Creation and the Adam and Eve story is about separation. Physical[1] and spiritual death are now introduced as our bodies and spirits will one day be separated just as we are currently separated from God's presence.[2]

The Greek word used for Atonement in the New Testament means "restoration to the divine."[3] True partnership between

Adam and Eve—man and woman, *'adam* and God—is divine.

As we return to the symbolism of Adam and Eve, we see parallels with Jesus Christ.

BRINGING FORTH LIFE

Adam leaves the garden, a place of honor where he walked and talked with Heavenly Father, in order to bring life to earth, to create bodies that will house the spirits waiting in heaven.[4] Had he and Eve not made the choice to partake of the fruit that would enable them to create those bodies, life would have stopped with them, and progress for the earth would have been halted as well.

Jesus Christ left His throne, His place of honor where He dwelt with Heavenly Father to rescue mankind, as well. Had he not descended from His paradise to lead by example and perform the Atonement, mankind would have been lost forever, never to return to a resurrected body back into the presence of a Heavenly Father; their progress would have been stopped forever.

Eve enters into the "valley of the shadow of death" as she brings forth life through childbirth. The Savior descended below all things, traveling through a very dark shadow near death as He suffered in the Garden of Gethsemane to bring forth life for all of us. Both endured unimaginable pain—Christ obviously more than hers, but she second only to Him.

Three beautiful acts of life occur in a garden: 1) Eve partakes of the fruit, allowing her body to now produce life; 2) Adam partakes of the fruit with the full knowledge he needs to do so in order to bring children into the world, to bring to pass *mankind*; 3) Jesus Christ offers the greatest act of sacrifice in all time and eternity, that of the Atonement—that one act that everything else in all of our history, including pre- and post-mortality, hinges upon. That one act that gives true life to all of humanity—both the spiritual and the physical, with a free gift of resurrection to all.

A COVERING OF PROTECTION

Luke 24:49 speaks of the disciples "endued with power from on high." *Endued* is a Greek word that means "endowed" or "clothed." In the Adam and Eve account, the Lord clothed them both in animal skins before they were driven out of the garden,[5] a better protection against the elements than the flimsy leaves. Besides the many lessons this act served for our first parents, it is also symbolic of the covering of the Atonement. This is one of the reasons that faithful endowed members of The Church of Jesus Christ of Latter-day Saints wear temple garments. It serves as "a reminder of the sacred covenants they have made with the Lord and also as a protection against temptation and evil. How it is worn is an outward expression of an inward commitment to follow the Savior."[6]

The power and promise of the Atonement of Jesus Christ is to bring back together that which has been separated; to bring *adam*—mankind—back into the presence of God, and to bring Adam and Eve together as one. "Until the woman and the man actually partake of the fruit, the use of plural Hebrew pronouns in the text indicates a union in their actions,"[7] meaning they were acting, working, and making decisions on their own. Their actions created the Fall—the separation from God. Christ's Atonement can bring back together what the Fall tore apart, to unite once again that which was divided, to overcome the separations mankind experienced—from God and from the masculine or feminine half.

The beauty of the Atonement is that it will make fair everything in this life that was unfair, unjust, and wrong. Eve's choice and the Fall itself changed the role of woman. She (and Adam) no longer enjoyed the autonomy they once had in the garden. What will equality and partnership look like in the hereafter for the obedient? We do not know the answer to that question. But the glory, beauty, and joy will defy all description.

PRAYING TO AND WAITING ON THE LORD

So what is a woman to do in this church and in the world? What if a woman sincerely feels marginalized or set aside, feels she is not able to experience all that she is capable of achieving because of her sex?

It is not cliché counsel to turn to God. Elder Todd Christofferson suggested, "We do not need to achieve some minimum level of capacity or goodness before God will help—divine aid can be ours every hour of every day, no matter where we are. . . . Beyond desiring His help, we must exert ourselves, repent, and choose God for Him to be able to act in our lives consistent with just and moral agency. . . . Simply take responsibility and go to work so that there is something for God to help us with."[8]

Elder Bednar also taught that "[Christ] can reach out, touch, succor, heal, and strengthen us to be more than we could ever be and help us to do that which we could never do relying only upon our own power."[9] Protests, murmuring, and arguing are very worldly ways to get a point across, to bring attention to a situation one may feel is very unfair. But Christ is always aware. If this gospel is indeed restored by a prophet, led by apostles and prophets under the direction of Christ, comfort can be found in the knowledge that He is speaking to them and that they are listening. The Atonement guarantees that our lives will eventually be made fair, but we must also be patient with the realization that some of this will be done within the Lord's timeline and not ours, and not in a way that the world may classify as "fair."

Through the Atonement, Jesus Christ suffered not just for sins, but also for fears, disappointment, injustices, and inequities that exist in the world and in our personal lives. This means that He can and will give us guidance and comfort regarding these inequities and the course we are to follow. As we adhere to our covenants He will provide direction to either remedy the situation[10] or to what is expected of us as we wait for the scales to be balanced. The Atonement enables us to do more and be better than what we previously achieved or conceived.

The Atonement of Jesus Christ is not the beginning, the middle, or the end. The Atonement is everything: it is through us, between us, by us; it is in our DNA cells, our souls, the air we breathe, and the energy around us.

Hold fast to covenants, waiting patiently upon the Lord. He provides peace of mind and faith that His plan for us is infinitely better than our plans for ourselves.

ENDNOTES

1. Alma 12:23
2. Alma 12:16,32
3. Strong, *Strong's Exhaustive Concordance*, Greek word 2643.
4. The Garden of Eden was a place that existed without time and thus would not allow the creation and growth of another human being—as to do so required time.
5. Genesis 3:21; Moses 4:27
6. First Presidency Letter, 1October 10, 1988, as quoted by Carlos E. Asay, "The Temple Garment, 'An Outward Expression of an Inward Commitment,'" ChurchofJesusChrist.org/study/liahona/1999/09/the-temple-garment-an-outward-expression-of-an-inward-commitment?lang=eng, accessed December 18, 2019.
7. Dawn Hall Anderson, Marie Cornwall, and Jolene Edmunds Rockwood, "Eve's Role in the Creation and the Fall to Mortality," in *Women and the Power within: to See Life Steadily and See It Whole* (Salt Lake City, UT: Deseret Book Co., 1991), 49–62.
8. D. Todd Christofferson, "Free Forever, to Act for Themselves," The Church of Jesus Christ of Latter-day Saints, October 2014, churchofjesuschrist.org/study/ensign/2014/11/saturday-morning-session/free-forever-to-act-for-themselves?lang=eng.
9. David A. Bednar, "Bear Up Their Burdens with Ease," The Church of Jesus Christ of Latter-day Saints, April 2014, https://www.churchofjesuschrist.org/study/ensign/2014/05/sunday-morning-session/bear-up-their-burdens-with-ease?lang=eng.
10. But we should always remember the counsel and avoid the temptation of steadying the ark.
11. Chronicles 13:9–12 and Doctrine &Covenants 85:8

Chapter 20

EQUALITY

Who is it that whispers so subtly in our ear that a gift given to another somehow diminishes the blessings we have received? Who makes us feel that if God is smiling on another, then He surely must somehow be frowning on us? You and I both know who does this—it is the father of all lies. It is Lucifer, our common enemy, whose cry down through the corridors of time is always and to everyone, "Give me thine honor"... But God does not work this way. The [F]ather... does not tantalize his children. He does not mercilessly measure them against their neighbors. He doesn't even compare them with each other. His gestures of compassion toward one do not require a withdrawal or denial of love for the other.... Toward both of his children [H]e extends charity.[1]

—Elder Jeffrey R. Holland

PROTECTING EVE

Spiritually speaking, there is no difference in equality between genders.[2] However, there are physical differences, and gender is divinely appointed by God and is essential to identity, mission, and purpose.[3]

Gender is more than just a mortal condition that can fluctuate or that ceases to exist after death. It is eternal and sacred, predetermined before birth,[4] and will continue after the Resurrection.[5] Blessings, gifts, responsibilities, and stewardships have been assigned to the genders, with the gift of agency of how to magnify and fulfill those stewardships. Heavenly Father loves each of His sons and daughters equally.

We are to understand that the narrative of the woman being created from the rib of man is symbolic and not historical. This narrative is to provide a foundation of *oneness and unity* for all husband-and-wife unions.

Adam himself states, "Therefore shall a man leave his father and his mother, and shall cleave unto his wife: and they shall be one flesh."[6] Adam recognizes that Eve is on equal standing with him. How can two entities be of one flesh and not be equal?

Once he realized that he had failed to protect Eve from harm, Adam likely vowed to be by her side from that day forward, doing his best to not repeat his mistake in the Garden of Eden. All of the sons of Adam must make those same vows, to do their best to protect all the daughters from Eve from abuse of any kind. Too much goes on behind closed doors, and the effects are far-reaching. No action or behavior is performed in a vacuum.

"The Family: A Proclamation to the World," states, "We warn that individuals who . . . abuse spouse or offspring, or who fail to fulfill family responsibilities will one day stand accountable before God."[7] Leaders who knowingly allow abusers to escape accountability will also one day answer to God.

LANGUAGE

Some of this disconnect would be vastly improved with a simple change in language and the use of titles. Why and how is language important? What difference do titles make? Former communist countries struggle to translate many spiritual and religious concepts from English to a native language. The communists, in their attempt to eradicate religion in the lives of the citizens, stripped many of the words associated with religion from books, practice, and speech. If a word for something doesn't exist, then that concept ceases to be relevant.[8]

We discussed the power and symbolism of titles and names in a previous chapter. Our temple ceremonies teach of their power and sacredness. Titles in the Church such as bishop, Relief Society president, minister, elder, and so on give a basic, foundational understanding of the role of the title bearer. Some of the language is simply missing because as a church, we don't know what to call people.

For instance, a temple president's wife is called the temple matron. From that title, we know what her role is and what her relationship is to the patrons, as well as to her husband, the president. But what about a mission president's wife? Could we start a cultural trend by referring to her as a mission matron? She moves out of the shadows and away from the reflection of the trailing spouse.

The Church's leadership—apostles and prophets—are acutely aware of this disconnect, and in the last several years have addressed this issue, especially in terms of language. Elder Faust, in his 1996 April general conference talk, stated, "Every father is to his family a patriarch and every mother a matriarch as coequals in their distinctive parental roles."[9]

The Church is definitely moving toward a more visible male/ female complementary duality in leadership roles. We see this in Church headquarters, as well as in local leadership roles, where leaders are modeling a true partnership of men and women, complementing each other's strengths and working to bless the lives of all members of the Church better together than they could separately.

ACCOUNTABILITY

So, between Adam and Eve, who is the most important in the Garden of Eden and thus, by extension, the most important in our mortal world, in our relationships, in our marriages? Nibley articulates this very well when he states, "There is no patriarchy or matriarchy in the Garden; the two supervise each other. . . . It is, if you will, a system of checks and balances in which each party is as distinct and independent in its sphere as are the departments of government under the Constitution—and just as dependent on each other."[10]

Bruce and Marie Hafen said, "The Restoration clarifies Eve's—and Adam's—choice as essential to the eternal progression of God's children. We honor rather than condemn what they did, and we see Adam and Eve as equal partners."[11]

In the Church's theology, one sex does not have an eternal advantage over the other.[12] Both sexes are accountable before and to each other. Any successful marriage will have both the husband and wife hearkening to each other, offering and accepting counsel, refraining from that which would damage the relationship.

Whatever culture we live in, the church we belong to, or family we inherited, in the eyes of God, women and men are equal.[13] Ultimately, both are accountable first—and foremost—to God.

Elder M. Russell Ballard stated, "Our Father in Heaven is generous with His power. All men and all women have access to this power for help in their lives. All who have made sacred covenants with the Lord and who honor those covenants are eligible to receive personal revelation, to be blessed by the ministering of angels, to commune with God, to receive the fullness of the gospel, and, ultimately, to become heirs alongside Jesus Christ of all our Father has."[14]

In our premortal life there were those who chose to follow the brightest light, that of Jesus Christ, the "self-existent one,"[15] the "I am." Those who chose to align with Heavenly Father's plan were given the opportunity of a "second life," this earthly life with a chance at a physical body and our next step on that path of exaltation to become like our Heavenly Parents.

The invitation to come to know Jesus Christ as their Savior, to obey, and repent are the same for both genders. Elder Dallin H. Oaks said, "Whoever exercises priesthood authority [male or female] should forget about their rights and concentrate on their responsibilities. That is a principle needed in society at large. The famous Russian writer Aleksandr Solzhenitsyn is quoted as saying,

'It is time . . . to defend not so much human rights as human obligations.' Latter-day Saints surely recognize that qualifying for exaltation is not a matter of asserting rights but a matter of fulfilling responsibilities."[16]

FOREORDINATION

Latter-day Saint leaders have consistently taught that Adam (and other priesthood holders) were foreordained for their specific missions on the earth. Adam's was to be the first man and to help initiate the Fall by partaking of the fruit.[17] Women, especially Eve, are also included in foreordained missions. Bruce R. McConkie taught, "Christ and Mary, Adam and Eve, Abraham and Sarah, and a host of mighty men and equally glorious women comprised that group of 'the noble and great ones,' to whom the Lord Jesus said: 'We will go down, for there is space there, and we will take of these materials, and we will make an earth whereon these may dwell' (Abraham 3:22–24)."[18]

As a side note, it is interesting to note that the Apocrypha of John referred to Eve as Sophia, indicating that was her name before coming to earth and taking upon herself the title and mission of Eve as "Life" and "the mother of the living, by the *foreknowledge*" (emphasis added).

Both men and women have missions associated with life-giving ordinances. To review, "ordinances are physical acts which signify or symbolize an underlying spiritual act."[19] The ordinances that Latter-day Saints are most familiar with are always performed by the authority of the priesthood and in the name of Jesus Christ. Though not official doctrine, it is the author's opinion that our pre-earth life and entrance into this mortal world most likely was performed with priesthood authority as well.

We can think of the first "ordinance" of birth as performed by the woman, the *priestess*. The *priest* (male) must stand aside and can only assist with support and prayers. The next ordinance on the covenant path of re-birth (baptism) is performed only by the *priest*, with now the *priestess* standing aside and merely assisting with support and prayers.

Author David Goates articulated it like this: "Remember, all mankind (all men, women, and children) must be born twice—or *'born again'*—to enter into eternal life. The first birth is physical and is performed only by the priestess. The second birth is spiritual (born of the spirit) and is performed only by the priest (baptism of water and of fire or spirit). Both are ultimately essential. . . . In both births the three fundamental elements of birth are present: the water, the blood, and the spirit."[20]

TEMPLE EQUALITY

Ida Smith wrote, "As temples were built and temple ordinances restored, our understanding of the male/female relationship has increased: Both men and women are conditionally sealed to become kings and queens, priests and priestesses. Both share the blessings of the priesthood. Both share the gifts of the spirit (i.e., to heal, to be healed, to speak in tongues, to prophesy, etc.)."[21]

Priesthood authority exercised by both men and women in the temple is often unrecognized by those both in and outside of the Church. The latter is understandable, but the former is not. "Latter-day Saints and others often mistakenly equate priesthood with religious office and the men who hold it, which obscures the broader Latter-day Saint concept of priesthood."[22] It bears repeating: priesthood is not a gender. It is an authority and power from God. Both men and women operate through, with, and under it.

Priesthood ordinances both inside and outside of the temple were restored to bless both men and women, allowing and enabling them to return to the presence of the Lord. We were all created, male and female, as beings of light in an atmosphere of love and learning.

Elder John A. Widstoe wrote that "this doctrine of equal rights is confirmed in the ordinances of the Church, which are alike for man and woman. Faith, repentance, and baptism are the same for all. The rewards, such as the gift of the Holy Ghost and the temple ordinances, are alike for men and women. The gifts and obligations of the gospel are alike for all. The man who holds the priesthood officiates in it, but the blessings of it descend upon the woman, also."[23]

What other philosophy or organization speaks so beautifully about the identity, purpose, and divinity of womanhood in such a way as the gospel of Jesus Christ?

ENDNOTES

1. Jeffrey R. Holland, "The Other Prodigal," The Church of Jesus Christ of Latter-day Saints, ChurchofJesusChrist.org/general-conference/2002/04/the-other-prodigal?lang=eng&_r=1, accessed December 18, 2019.
2. Galations 3:28
3. "The Family: A Proclamation to the World," ChurchofJesusChrist.org/topics/family-proclamation?lang=eng&_r=1
4. "For I, the Lord God, created all things . . . spiritually, before they were naturally upon the face of the earth" (Moses 3:4–7).
5. "The Family: A Proclamation to the World." See also James E. Talmage, "The Eternity of Sex," Young Woman's Journal, Oct. 1914, ontentdm.lib.byu.edu/digital/collection/YWJ/id/17256/, accessed December 18, 2019.
6. Genesis 2:24
7. "The Family: A Proclamation to the World"
8. Sharon Eubank, "'This Is a Woman's Church.'" FairMormon, August 8, 2014, fairmormon.org/perspectives/fair-conferences/2014–fairmormon-conference/womans-church.
9. James E. Faust, "The Prophetic Voice," The Church of Jesus Christ of Latter-day Saints, ChurchofJesusChrist.org/general-conference/1996/04/the-prophetic-voice?lang=eng, accessed December 18, 2019.
10. Hugh Nibley, "Patriarchy and Matriarchy," Old Testament and Related Studies, vol. 1 in The Collected Works of Hugh Nibley (Salt Lake City: Deseret Book and Foundation for Ancient Research & Mormon Studies [FARMS], 1986). Neal A. Maxwell institute for Religious Scholarship
11. Bruce C. Hafen and Marie K. Hafen, "Crossing Thresholds and Becoming Equal Partners," The Church of Jesus Christ of Latter-day Saints, August 2007, churchofjesuschrist.org/study/

liahona/2007/08/crossing-thresholds-and-becoming-equal-part-ners?lang=eng

12. See for instance, Valerie M. Hudson and Richard B. Miller, "Equal Partnership in Marriage," The Church of Jesus Christ of Latter-day Saints, ChurchofJesusChrist.org/ensign/2013/04/equal-partner-ship-in-marriage?lang=eng, accessed December 10, 2019.

13. Dallin H. Oaks, "The Keys and Authority of the Priesthood," The Church of Jesus Christ of Latter-day Saints, April 2014, churchofjesuschrist.org/study/general-conference/2014/04/the-keys-and-authority-of-the-priesthood?lang=eng&_r=1

14. M. Russell Ballard, "Men and Women and Priesthood Power," The Church of Jesus Christ of Latter-day Saints, September 2014, ChurchofJesusChrist.org/ensign/2014/09/men-and-women-and-priesthood-power?lang=eng

15. James Edward Talmage, in *Jesus the Christ; a Study of the Messiah and His Mission According to Holy Scriptures Both Ancient and Modern* (Salt Lake City, UT: Deseret Book, 1970), 36, ChurchofJesusChrist.org/manual/old-testament-student-man-ual-genesis-2–samuel/enrichment-section-a-who-is-the-god-of-the-old-testament?lang=eng

16. Oaks, ibid.

17. Brigham Young, 3 June 1855, *Journal of Discourses*, 2:302.

18. Bruce R. McConkie, "Eve and the Fall," in *Woman* (Salt Lake City, Utah: Deseret Book, 1979), 59.

19. en.wikipedia.org/wiki/Ordinance_(Latter_Day_Saints)

20. thegoateskids.blogspot.com/2009/11/chapter-sixteen-patriar-chal-order-of.html

21. Ida Smith, "The Lord as a Role Model for Men and Women," The Church of Jesus Christ of Latter-day Saints, ChurchofJe-susChrist.org/ensign/1980/08/the-lord-as-a-role-model-for-men-and-women?lang=eng, accessed December 18, 2019.

22. "Joseph Smith's Teachings about Priesthood, Temple, and Women," The Church of Jesus Christ of Latter-day Saints, ChurchofJesusChrist.org/topics/joseph-smiths-teachings-about-priesthood-temple-and-women?lang=eng#40, accessed December 18, 2019.

23. John A. Widtsoe, in *Joseph Smith: Seeker after Truth, Prophet of God* (Salt Lake City, UT: Bookcraft, 1993), 185.

Chapter 21
LED BY A LIVING PROPHET

Look unto me in every thought;
doubt not, fear not.

—Doctrine and Covenants 6:36

DELIBERATE QUESTIONS
AND CORRECT SOURCES

For some individuals, certain elements of the Adam and Eve story feel troubling. We live in a temporal world that by design must be lived in, through, with, and by faith. Knowing that, some may wonder, is it okay to question? What is my role? What changes am I allowed to bring to the culture? What narrative is appropriate?

It is certainly appropriate and encouraged to search for answers, to seek for more understanding to those principles, doctrines, or matters in the Church or gospel that may confuse or unsettle us. This is at the heart of gaining a testimony. The Holy Ghost can and will testify of truth. But as a word of caution, in the search for truth, *correct sources* are necessary for correct answers. Contrary to popular belief, the internet is not the font of all knowledge. Ask questions, but keep the focus on correct principles.

Joseph Smith's quest for wisdom and knowledge is a perfect template for anyone seeking answers. The Holy Ghost must be present, and in order to invite Him, one must approach those questions with a commitment of respect, as well as using the doctrine of The Church of Jesus Christ of Latter-day Saints as a touchstone. Go to the right sources. Trust the prophets rather than the internet alone. But most of all, be patient and humble.

Sharon Eubank promised:

> We know so little about what the Lord is doing with men and women and their respective roles with the priesthood, but He will teach us here a little, there a little, precept on precept,[1] as we are able to understand and comprehend. As we continue forward with faith in those things we wish we had more understanding, the Lord will continue to bless us, opening our eyes of understanding, increasing our faith, and deepening our assurances that we are engaged in a good cause; that "this is the right place and the right doctrine."[2]

We can be steadfast in the cause, staying true to what the Holy Ghost has revealed to us. Only by keeping covenants and the commandments are we protected from deception.

When receiving answers and accepting guidance, individuals are wise to always *consider the source*. What knowledge are we seeking, and where are we searching? What is the spirit that enters the heart when a specific source offers answers? What is the spirit in *our* heart as we seek for these answers concerning our specific mission in life?

WORKING AND SERVING WITHIN THE CULTURE

There is nothing wrong with working to make things better within the culture of the Church; learning to work with each other, expressing and recognizing the value of men and women, and listening to the concerns of women in the Church are worthwhile pursuits. There are not (yet) answers to everything, but as we work toward a more harmonious and equal relationship between men and women, we can choose to keep our faith and remain steadfast in our testimonies as we prepare ourselves to receive more truth and light.

Patricia Holland articulated it well when she said, "We should seek diligently and prayerfully the light that would quicken our hearts and minds to truly *desire* the outcomes we make in righteous decisions. Our prayers ought to be to see as God sees, to flip the switch in our minds so we may see things eternally. If we listen too often to the voices of the world, we will become confused and tainted. We must anchor ourselves in the spirit and that requires daily vigilance."[3]

SOME THOUGHTS ON THE SEARCH

Once in awhile, one comes across a scripture that may have little personal relevance—such as Mosaic laws that were applicable only to a specific time, place, and people—and yet may contain good basic principles for any Christian. The following are some suggestions on gleaning messages and personal value from scripture, despite the cultural constraints:

1. Focus on truths and doctrines rather than cultural mores. When a question arises or doubts surface, always go to the source: scriptures, prophets, and apostles. Avoid hyper-focusing on a single passage or verse, especially at the expense of the entire sermon.

2. Certain counsel is given for a specific period, time, and people. Paul, a Jew with Roman citizenship who converted to Christianity, well understood the strong cultural underpinnings of the new branches he was teaching in his day. There were many cultural undercurrents of the Saints that he had to work with, one of which was the subordination of the female members. He knew that full conversion and transition takes time and effort.

3. Take the scriptural context into account, noting that occasionally, the Lord adjusts His instructions. The

priesthood was first given only to the tribe of Levi.[4] In our day, it is given to every worthy male.[5] While God is the same yesterday, today, and forever, we are not. We are growing and changing, and depending on our growth, there is a time and a place for everything.[6]

4. If there are questions, continue to search and pray, but in the meantime, avoid "steadying the ark." As Bruce R. McConkie counseled, "stay in the mainstream of the church."[7]

5. Follow this three-prong test for interpreting scripture and deciding how it pertains to one personally: "Is my interpretation in harmony with (1) the teachings of the standard works, (2) the modern prophets, and (3) the witness of the Holy Ghost?"[8]

President Spencer W. Kimball added: "I have learned that where there is a prayerful heart, a hungering after righteousness, a forsaking of sins, and obedience to the commandments of God, the Lord pours out more and more light until there is finally power to pierce the heavenly veil and to know more than man knows. A person of such righteousness has the priceless promise that one day he shall see the Lord's face and know that he is."[9]

At the churchofjesuschrist.org website, we read the following quote about acquiring spiritual knowledge: "During times when we may not immediately find answers to our questions, it is helpful to remember that although Heavenly Father has revealed all that is necessary for our salvation, He has not yet revealed all truth. As we continue to seek for answers, we must live by faith—trusting that we will eventually receive the answers we seek. As we are faithful to the truth and light we have already received, we will receive more. Answers to our questions and prayers often come 'line upon line, precept upon precept.'"[10]

PATIENCE IN THE QUEST FOR ANSWERS

There are no shortcuts, only the old-fashioned method of toil and labor: the expended effort of learning the gospel and the challenge of living it. So we search and ask the right questions from the right sources. Then what? If even after that open-minded process, certain events and policies continue to cause consternation and confusion, Elder Jeffrey R. Holland offers comfort: "When those moments come and issues surface, the resolution of which is not immediately forthcoming, *hold fast to what you already know and stand strong until additional knowledge comes.*"[11]

This is the choice we face. Do we stay with what we have felt and been taught by the Holy Ghost?[12] There are not always immediate answers to everything. Not in this life. But the Holy Ghost is real. God is real, and so are His servants.

The bottom line is that there is one man who may receive revelation regarding the entire Church as a collective whole, and that is the prophet. In the Old Testament we read: "If there be a prophet among you, I the Lord will make myself known unto him. . . . With him will I speak mouth to mouth."[13]

While it is healthy and normal to engage in respectful dialogue, there must be caution with the intent of that dialogue. False ideas can and have been confused with the Holy Ghost, as Miriam and Aaron attempted to convince Moses he needed to share his authority with them.[14] But through obedience to the commandments and keeping covenants, we will not be deceived. Discernment will be gifted so that the precepts of man can be distinguished from those of God. It is Jesus Christ who is the head of this church, with the prophet as His mouthpiece. It is possible to trust in the plan and still seek for answers.

There is an eternal nature of our individual identities, and our gender plays an integral part of our personalities. Spencer W. Kimball lovingly counseled, "You need, more and more, to feel the perfect love which our Father in Heaven has for you and to sense the value he places upon you as an individual. Ponder upon these great truths, especially in those moments when (in the stillness of such anxiety as you may experience as an individual) you might otherwise wonder and be perplexed."[15]

THE BIG PICTURE

God gives us time to make shifts in our thinking, to rearrange how we think the puzzle pieces can and will fit together. God's ways are better than our ways. His time frame is different from ours. Faith is moving forward with patience as we wait for the continuing revelation to unfold.

Male or female, married or single, all must increase in their knowledge of the Savior's teachings and in their testimony of the Atonement. All are equal in that quest and responsibility. It affects how we perform our duties and our partnerships.

"Sometimes to be tested and proved requires that we be temporarily deprived," Spencer W. Kimball has said, "but righteous women and men will one day receive all . . . that our Father has! It is not only worth waiting for; it is worth living for!"[16]

Elder Uchtdorf said, "Obedience is not so much the process of bending, twisting, and pounding our souls into something we are not. Instead, it is the process by which we discover what we truly are made of."[17]

Keep working. Keep serving. Keep faithful to covenants and ordinances. All questions will be answered, and puzzles will be worked out to reveal a marvelous, awe-inspiring mosaic.

ENDNOTES

1. 2 Nephi 28:30
2. Sharon Eubank, "This is a Woman's Church", FAIR Conference, August 8, 2014, fairmormon.org/perspectives/fair-conferences/2014-fairmormon-conference/womans-church
3. Patricia T. Holland, "A Woman's Perspective on the Priesthood," The Church of Jesus Christ of Latter-day Saints, churchofjesuschrist.org/study/liahona/1982/06/a-womans-perspective-on-the-priesthood?lang=eng, accessed December 19, 2019.
4. Doctrine and Covenants 84:18; Numbers 8:11–15
5. Doctrine and Covenants Official Declaration 2, ChurchofJesusChrist.org/scriptures/dc-testament/od/2?lang=eng
6. Ecclesiastes 3:1–8

7. Bruce R. McConkie and Mark L. McConkie, in *Doctrines of the Restoration: Sermons & Writings of Bruce R. McConkie* (Salt Lake City, UT: Bookcraft, 1989), 67.

8. George A. Horton, "How Can We Tell Which Scriptures Can Be Likened to All of Us and Which Ones Cannot?," churchofjesuschrist.org/study/ensign/1994/01/i-have-a-question/how-can-we-tell-which-scriptures-can-be-likened-to-all-of-us-and-which-ones-cannot.html?lang=eng, accessed December 17, 2019.

9. Spencer W. Kimball, "Give the Lord Your Loyalty," *Ensign*, March 1980, 4.

10. "Acquiring Spiritual Knowledge, *Doctrinal Mastery Core Document*, 2016, ChurchofJesusChrist.org, churchofjesuschrist.org/study/liahona/2016/11/news-of-the-church/doctrinal-mastery?lang=eng. See also Proverbs 3:5–6; Ether 12:6, 2 Nephi 28:30.

11. Jeffrey R. Holland, "Lord, I Believe," *Ensign*, May 2013, 94; Doctrine and Covenants 6:36.

12. Bonnie Oscarson as quoted in Sharon Eubank's "Being a Woman: An Eternal Perspective", *Ensign*, August 2016.

13. Numbers 12:6, 8

14. It is important to note that this experience is not about a woman trying to usurp the power of a man, but speaking to one without authority—in this case, both a man and a woman—attempting to claim authority that did not belong to them.

15. Spencer W. Kimball, ChurchofJesusChrist.org/manual/teachings-spencer-w-kimball/chapter-20?lang=eng.

16. Spencer W. Kimball, *Ensign*, November 1979, 102–3.

17. Dieter F. Uchtdorf, "He Will Place You on His Shoulders and Carry You Home," The Church of Jesus Christ of Latter-day Saints, ChurchofJesusChrist.org/general-conference/2016/04/he-will-place-you-on-his-shoulders-and-carry-you-home?lang=eng.

Chapter 22

A LOVE STORY

*Turn it this way, turn it that way, for
everything is in it. Pore over it, grow old
and gray over it. Do not stir from it, for
you can have no better portion than it.*

—Avot 5:22[1]

The story of Adam and Eve is nothing less than a love story. God created the male first, placing him in the garden alone for a time. Why did He not just create both male and female at the same time? God Himself states that man should not be alone, and we see that after Eve partakes of the fruit, Adam, having already experienced loneliness before God introduced him to Eve, decides to follow her.

While he recognized the wisdom in partaking the fruit and leaving the garden, Adam also had an overwhelming desire to remain with Eve in a pain-riddled mortal world rather than exist alone in the garden. He ate the fruit, despite the consequences, so as to bring happiness to the *isha* who brought him life.

"JOY—AND KNOWLEDGE—COMES FROM PARTICIPATION IN CHANGE"[2]

One of the touching moments in the narrative of Adam and Eve is their unified recognition that the Fall was a blessing, and that neither blamed the other. Moses 5 shows us the depth of their partnership: working in the field together, praying and worshiping together, teaching the gospel to their children together, hearing the voice of the Lord together. They had learned their lesson in the garden about the follies and danger of just living as roommates and doing their own thing. Through their eternal sealing in the garden by the Father and through their mortal experiences—including the pain, sorrows, and trials—they became of one heart and one mind.

Yes, Adam would have been content for both of them to remain in the garden. Eve, for reasons she did not yet fully know, had a yearning for something more, a yearning to be the Mother of all Living.

In Moses we read of the change that fatherhood (and motherhood) caused: "Blessed be the name of God, for because of my transgression my eyes are opened, and in this life I shall have joy, and again in the flesh I shall see God. And Eve, his wife, heard all these things and was glad, saying: Were it not for our transgression we never should have had seed, and never should have known good and evil, and the joy of our redemption, and the eternal life which God giveth unto all the obedient."[3]

Adam is bound to Mother Eve, soon to comprehend through experience the magnitude of cleaving, willing to follow her and suffer with her.[4]

LOVE VERSUS WESTERN ROMANCE

Adam and Eve essentially had an arranged marriage. It's difficult to look at their situation and relationship through an accurate lens. In most Western societies there exists a powerful "cult of romance," where many struggle between two ideals: romance and commitment. Just a quick glance through a Hollywood tabloid reveals the fickle side of many relationships. The message that we are constantly bombarded with is the search for one's soul mate. The lie that is perpetuated is that the way to find one's *own* soul is through romance.

This becomes one of the great paradoxes of our time. Romantic love tends to be viewed as intense and adventurous. It is the antithesis of a human, normal, down-to-earth, day-to-day relationship.

The best way to describe the type of love that Adam and Eve likely achieved, and what we can achieve by extension, is what Robert Johnson calls "stirring-the-oatmeal" kind of love. It demonstrates the difference between romantic love and human love:

> Stirring the oatmeal is a humble act—not exciting or thrilling. But it symbolizes a relatedness that brings love down to earth. It represents a willingness to share ordinary human life, to find meaning in the simple, and romantic tasks: earning a living, living within a budget, putting out the garbage, feeding the baby in the middle of the night. To "stir the oatmeal" means to find the relatedness, the value, even the beauty, and simple and ordinary things, not to eternally demand a cosmic drama, and entertainment, or an extraordinary intensity and everything. Like the rice hulling of the Zen monks, the spinning wheel of Gandhi, the tent making of St. Paul, it represents the discovery of the sacred in the midst of the humble and ordinary.[5]

Many couples feel that in order to save their marriage they need to return to the time in their relationship that felt exciting, romantic, and thrilling. Erroneously they struggle accepting each other as two ordinary, imperfect human beings, and accepting him or her as enough. The entire idea of romance or "being in love" is—albeit common—childlike and immature, but it is not necessary for a successful, fulfilling, and happy relationship.

So, what is *love*?

One of the root problems with the *in love* versus *love* relationship is humility and meekness. Elder David A. Bednar said, "Humility generally denotes dependence upon God and the constant need for His guidance and support, a distinguishing characteristic of meekness is a particular spiritual receptivity to learning both from the Holy Ghost and from [other] people."[6]

To be a true love story, the spouse should always take first place, preeminent and above all other pursuits, hobbies, careers, and relationships. Spouses must create a relationship on the foundation of equality. Valerie Hudson said, "The first utterance Adam made after God created him and Eve in the Garden of Eden was to declare Eve's equality with him—that they would be 'one flesh.'"[7]

Elder Uchtdorf taught that "those who save their marriages understand that this pursuit takes time, patience, and, above all, the blessings of the Atonement of Jesus Christ."[8]

To love someone else is to be willing to sacrifice one's ego for the good of the relationship. It is the surge of warmth for another person as small acts are performed in what may appear as the daily mundane.

Love is an act of growing up, seeing and accepting realistic expectations of others.

To love is to value and appreciate another person for who she or he is.

To love is not even waiting for that surge of warmth before serving, for a mature person has already realized that most often, an action must be taken before the love is to grow and flourish.

To love is no longer placing one's happiness or mood on the shoulders of another. It is our own burden, and right, to carry.

In the end we will realize that what has been needed in our relationships and culture is not so much to be loved, but rather to love. To be *in love* is a phase. To *love* is a power.

BEST FRIENDS

"When a man and a woman are truly friends, they know each other's difficult points and weaknesses," Johnson writes. "But they are not inclined to stand in judgment on them. They are more concerned with helping each other and enjoying each other than they are with finding fault. . . . They want to affirm rather than to judge; they don't coddle, but neither do they dwell on our inadequacies. Friends back each other up in the tough times, help each other with the sordid and ordinary tasks of life. They don't impose impossible standards on each other, they don't ask for perfection, and they help each other rather than grind each other down with demands."[9]

Friendship in a marital relationship takes the artificiality out, replacing the impossible standards with something much more enduring and real.

The cultural ideal of Adam and Eve's day was designed and initiated by God: staying and working together in a marriage that did not end with death (for in the garden there was no death.) From the time of the Fall both parents were determined and committed—from that time forward—to obey all of Heavenly Father's commandments and to live as partners.

Friends settle comfortably into the ordinary, looking forward to spending time together in a life filled with glorious uncertainty, wondrous imperfection, and magnificent flaws. The goal was never to see how to change one another, but how to best enjoy each other. Husbands and wives truly can be friends with one another, unafraid of the simple and ordinary.

WE ARE ALL IN HIS IMAGE

The knowledge of our parentage opens the path to self-understanding and authenticity. We are children of Heavenly parents, and our potential to become like them one day is awesome. But consider the interchange of God becoming like man in order to reclaim humanity. Think of the message this sends as it relates to our earth life and our own love story.

Johnson wrote:

> God [Jesus Christ] came into the physical world and redeemed it; God becomes human! The implications of this belief, taken as symbol, are enormous," Johnson writes. "It means that this physical world, this physical body, and this mundane life we lead on this earth are also holy. It means that our fellow human beings have their own intrinsic value: they are not here merely to reflect our fantasy of a more perfect world or to carry our projections of anime or to join us and acting out an allegory of another world. The physical, mundane, ordinary world has its own beauty, its own validity, and its own laws to be observed. . . . The way to enlightenment, to soul, is not through the clouds, not by denying this earth. It is found within this mortal life, within the simplicity of our mundane tasks in our relationships with ordinary people.[10]

Heavenly Father wants us to become as He is, to have the kind of relationship He has with our Heavenly Mother. But in the meantime, while we are here on earth, let's make this time holy as well, and our relationships along with it.

THEIR LAST SEPARATION

In the pseudepigraphical[11] writings of Adam and Eve are the poignant accounts of their deaths. The reader can clearly see the transformations that have come upon our first parents, how they have lived a full life through their children—great joy as well as sorrow and deep pain. But the most tender writings are the accounts of Adam's impending death and Eve contemplating a life without him.

In a poignant account when he realizes his time is ending, Adam gathers his family: "But when our father Adam saw them around him, he wept at having to be separated from them."[12]

In these same works[13] we read of Eve's devastation when she realizes that Adam's days were coming to a close: "And when she saw him [Adam] weeping, Havah herself began to weep. 'My husband Adam, rise, give me half of your illness and let me bear it! . . . Why are you dying and I live? And how long have I to live after you die? Tell me.'"[14]

The account continues with Eve weeping and praying upon Adam's death until an angel comes to her side and beckons her to look up. As she gazes into heaven she sees a chariot of light, pulled by four "radiant eagles" and escorted by angels. She watches as the angels surround Adam's body, now lying in paradise. The angels pray over the body, asking, "Forgive him, O Father of all, for he is in your image."[15]

We are not sure how much longer Eve lived after her husband's death, but the Apocrypha makes note of her sorrow as she waits. Halevi wrote, "While living, she herself wept about her death, because she did not know where her body was to be placed. And Havah, in the hour of her death, implored that she might be buried where Adam her husband was, saying, 'My master, Lord and God of all excellence, do not separate me from the body of Adam.'"[16]

> Just as I was with him in Paradise
> we were together in the Garden
> and not separated,
> were not separate from one another
> so also let no one separate us now.
> Just as in life, so in [our] death.
> Let me be buried with him.[17]

The ending came quicker than they anticipated. The Adam and Eve story, and the potential of the patriarchal order, were both created for the sake of love: love first shared by our Heavenly Parents through providing mortal bodies and a Savior, and by giving us a real chance of having what they have. From Them, and with each other, we can experience eternal love.

ENDNOTES

1. Avot is a tractate (treatise or dissertation) of the Mishnah (compilation of Jewish law and part of the Talmud). It is the most popular and most cited Jewish texts. They are written in the style of the Wisdom Literature, such as Proverbs and Ecclesiastes. Avot is often called *Pirkei Avot*, "the Chapters of the Fathers." It is a compilation of ethical teachings and short sayings attributed to rabbis who lived at the beginning of the Common Era (CE) (myjewish-learning.com/article/pirkei-avot-ethics-of-our-fathers/).

2. Shira Halevi, in *The Life Story of Adam and Havah: a New Targum of Genesis 1:26–5:5* (Aronson, 1997), 192.

3. Moses 5:10–11

4. Hugh Nibley, "Patriarchy and Matriarchy," *Old Testament and Related Studies*, vol. 1 in *The Collected Works of Hugh Nibley* (Salt Lake City: Deseret Book Company and Foundation for Ancient Research & Mormon Studies [FARMS], 1986, Neal A. Maxwell institute for Religious Scholarship. See also Moses 4:23.

5. Robert A. Johnson, in *We: Understanding the Psychology of Romantic Love* (New York: Harper, 2013), 195.

6. David A. Bednar, "Meek and Lowly of Heart," April 2018, The church of Jesus Christ of Latter-day Saints, ChurchofJesusChrist.org/general-conference/2018/04/meek-and-lowly-of-heart?lang=eng

7. Valerie Hudson and Richard B. Miller, "Equal Partnership in Marriage," *Ensign*, April 2013, ChurchofJesusChrist.org/ensign/2013/04/equal-partnership-in-marriage?lang=eng

8. Dieter F. Uchtdorf, "In Praise of Those Who Save," April 2016, The Church of Jesus Christ of Latter-day Saints, ChurchofJesusChrist.org/general-conference/2016/04/in-praise-of-those-who-save?lang=eng

9. Johnson, 197.

10. Johnson, 143.

11. "The Pseudepigrapha [are] 52 texts written between 200 BC and AD 200 but ascribed to various prophets and kings in the Hebrew scriptures; many are apocalyptic in nature (thefreedictionary.com/pseudepigraphical).

12. DR S. C. MALAN, in *BOOK OF ADAM AND EVE: Also Called the Conflict of Adam and Eve with Satan, a Book of the Early... Eastern Church, Translated from the Ethiopic, With* (Place of publication not identified: FORGOTTEN Books, 2016), 114.

13. Ibid.; *The Apocalypse of Moses, Vita Adae*

14. Halevi, 285–6.

15. Ibid., 287.

16. Ibid., 289.

17. This is a combination of two accounts, the top line from Vita Adae and The Apocalypse of Moses as written in Shira Halevi's The Life Story of Adam and Havah; the second line from the Armenian translation of The Life of Adam and Eve.

APPENDIX

Temples are considered the most sacred places on earth to members of The Church of Jesus Christ of Latter-day Saints. Members think of temples literally as houses of the Lord. In these buildings, members in good standing receive the holiest ordinances available and make sacred covenants with God. Members also are able to perform vicarious service on behalf of their deceased ancestors, including baptism.[1]

Marriages that are performed with the God-ordained authority in the temple are *sealed*, meaning that the relationships are forever, that not even death can separate them.[2] Any children that are born after this sealing are considered sealed to their parents forever as well.

A temple or eternal marriage is one of the requirements for exaltation, which is to live with and as Heavenly Father and Mother.[3]

Temples are a place of divine sanctuary, where one can feel closer to Jesus Christ and Heavenly Father, learn more about one's purpose here on earth, and given instruction and spiritual guidance in how to become more like our Savior and Heavenly Father.

For a virtual tour and explanations of temples, please visit churchofjesuschrist.org/temples/rome-italy-temple-virtual-tour. Additional information about temples and the ordinances performed inside can also be found at churchofjesuschrist.org/temples?lang=eng.

ENDNOTES

1. See 1 Corinthians 15:29, 55–57; Matthew 3:15–17; John 3:2,5; Doctrine and Covenants 20:73–74, 22:4; www.lds.org/temples/what-is-proxy-baptism?lang=eng
2. "It is the same power that Jesus bestowed upon His Apostles during His ministry on earth" (Matthew 16:19), churchofjesus-christ.org/temples/what-happens-in-a-temple-sealing?lang=eng
3. See Doctrine and Covenants 131:1–3; 132:19.

ABOUT THE AUTHOR

Ramona Siddoway has published extensively in the United States, Europe, and Africa. Her writing has been translated into several languages around the world. Her favorite assignment was writing about the endangered Palanca Negra Antelope in West Africa. She traveled with a conservation group to a private Angolan reserve, camped out under the African stars, and interviewed local tribesman.

Whether writing or teaching, she is known for her wit and impeccable research. A graduate of Brigham Young University, Ramona is married with four adult children and seven grandchildren. She is a community organizer and grassroots activist on many fronts. She feels a responsibility to be an active member of both the local and global community. She is an avid reader, certified yoga instructor, and Texas homesteader. She breathes easier when she is nestled among the trees. Along with nonfiction, she writes quirky mystery.

Scan to visit

www.ramonasiddoway.com